Scott Foresman

Reading

Grade 2

Phonics Take-Home Readers

Scott Foresman
Phonics System

Scott Foresman

Editorial Offices: Glenview, Illinois • New York, New York
Sales Offices: Reading, Massachusetts • Duluth, Georgia • Glenview, Illinois
Carrollton, Texas • Menlo Park, California

Editorial Offices
Glenview, Illinois • New York, New York

Sales Offices
Reading, Massachusetts • Duluth, Georgia • Glenview, Illinois
Carrollton, Texas • Menlo Park, California

ISBN 0-673-61259-7

5 6 7 8 9 10-CRK-06 05 04 03 02 01

TABLE OF CONTENTS

Phonics Readers for Unit 1

Book 1   **The Fox and the Crow: An Aesop Fable**
Short *a, i, u; l, r,* and *s* blends

Book 2   **When Hen Went Shopping**
Short *e, o;* Final consonant blends

Book 3   **Check Out These Animals!**
Long vowels with final *e;* Initial consonant digraphs

Book 4   **Sweet Pea, the Black Sheep**
Long *e* spelled *ea, ee;* Final consonant digraphs

Book 5   **The Oldest Car in Merry County**
Long *e* spelled *e, y;* Inflected ending *-ed* (without spelling change)

Phonics Readers for Unit 2

Book 6   **Quail for Dinner**
Long *a* spelled *a, ai, ay;* Inflected endings *-es, -ing, -s* (without spelling change)

Book 7   **Fly High!**
Long *i* spelled *i, igh, y;* Medial consonants (include double medial consonants)

Book 8   **The Pond**
R-controlled vowels (*er, ir, ur*); Plurals *-s* and *-es* (including changing *y* to *i* before adding *-es*)

Book 9   **A Day in the Life of a Firefighter**
Long *o* spelled *o, oa, ow, oe;* Compound words

Book 10   **The Town Mouse and the Country Mouse**
Words with *ce, ge, se;* Possessives (singular and plural)

Phonics Readers for Unit 3

Book 11   **Out and About on the *Mayflower***
Vowel diphthongs *ou, ow;* Inflected endings (doubling final consonants before *-ed, -ing*)

Book 12   **Just Start**
R-controlled vowel (*ar*); Inflected endings (dropping *e* before *-ed, -ing*)

Book 13   **Have You Seen the New Newts?**
Vowel patterns *ew, oo, ou;* Contractions

Book 14   **Orlando**
R-controlled vowels (*or, ore, oor, our*); Inflected endings (changing *y* to *i* before *-ed, -es*)

Book 15   **What Could It Be?**
Vowel patterns *oo, ou;* Comparative endings *-er, -est*

Phonics Readers for Unit 4

Book 16 **Timmy's Ears**
R-controlled vowels (*ear, eer*);
Suffix -*ly*

Book 17 **Joyce, Who Hated Noise**
Vowel diphthongs *oi, oy*; Suffix
-*ful*

Book 18 **The Gingerbread Bakers**
Short *e* spelled *ea*; Suffix -*er*

Book 19 **The Best Baseball Players**
/ȯ/ vowel patterns (*al, au*); Silent
letter patterns (*gh, kn, mb*)

Book 20 **Fawn at Dawn**
/ȯ/ vowel patterns (*aw, ough*);
Silent letter patterns (*gn, wh, wr*)

Phonics Readers for Unit 5

Book 21 **Touchdown at Space Camp**
Short *u* spelled *ou*; Multisyllabic
words

Book 22 **Paul and His Blue Ox**
Schwa sound; Plurals -*s* and -*es*

Book 23 **The Statue of Liberty**
Vowel digraph *ue*; Schwa sound
in *weather*

Book 24 **Great Sunday Sleigh Rides**
Long *a* spelled *ei*; Multisyllabic
words (words with endings
and suffixes)

Book 25 **Extinct!**
Vowel pattern *ex*; Prefixes *un-,
dis-, re-*

Phonics Readers for Unit 6

Book 26 **Herbie and the Donkey**
Long *e* spelled *ie, ey*; Consonant
patterns *gh, ph, lf* /f/

Book 27 **The Shoemaker and the Elves**
Long *e* spelled *ei*; Plural -*es*
(changing *f* to *v* before adding)

Book 28 **Little Book of Bridges**
R-controlled vowels (*air, are*);
Consonant pattern *dge*/j/

Book 29 **The Broken Radio Jug Band**
Long vowels at the ends of
syllables; Consonants *ch* /k/ and
sch /sk/

Book 30 **Our Vacation**
R-controlled vowels (*ear* /ėr/, *our*
/our/); Syllable pattern *tion*

Scott Foresman
Reading

Grade 2
Phonics Reader 1

The Fox and the Crow:
An Aesop Fable
retold by Robert Newell
illustrated by
Manuel King

Phonics Skills:
• Short *a, i, u*
• *l, r,* and *s* blends

Scott Foresman
Phonics System

Scott Foresman

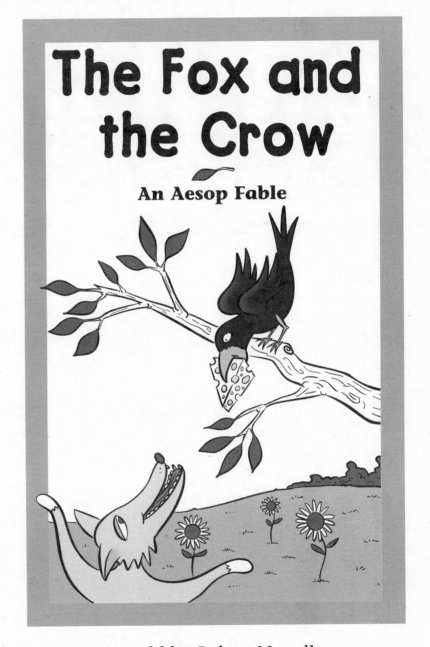

The Fox and the Crow

An Aesop Fable

retold by Robert Newell
illustrated by Manuel King

This book belongs to

_____

Phonics for Families: This book provides practice in reading the high-frequency words *could, have, need,* and *was.* It also provides practice reading words with the short vowel sounds *a, i, u* and words that begin with two blended consonants, such as *cr* in *crow* or *bl* in *black.* Read the book together with your child and then talk about how the fox tricked the crow.

Phonics Skills: Short *a, i, u; l, r,* and *s* blends

High-Frequency Words: *could, have, need, was*

Now what does this story tell us?

**Do not
let a fox
use sweet talk
to trick you!**

The Fox and the Crow

An Aesop Fable

retold by Robert Newell
illustrated by Manuel King

Scott Foresman

Editorial Offices: Glenview, Illinois • New York, New York
Sales Offices: Reading, Massachusetts • Duluth, Georgia
Glenview, Illinois • Carrollton, Texas • Menlo Park, California

One sunny day, Fox went for a run.

And when she did, the cheese
dropped out of her beak!
Fox grinned. He grabbed the
cheese. Then off he ran.

She opened her beak wide.
"CRAWK! CRAWK! CRAWK!"
she cried.

"Sniff, sniff. My nose is telling me something," said Fox. "What is that smell?"

His nose led him to a house. Up on the porch was a big chunk of cheese.

Fox jumped once. He jumped twice.
He had to have that cheese.

"Crr, crr, crr!" said Crow.
Fox started to walk away.
Crow could not stand it.
She had to show him.

© Scott Foresman 2

"Too bad you have such a small voice," Fox added.

"Please! Don't feel bad. Queens need to have a big voice, you know. And you just don't have one."

Then down flew Crow.
Flap! Snap!
Crow had it in her beak.

Now, this was not funny! Fox just
had to have that cheese.
Fox was tricky. Soon he had a
plan. He smiled.

"You know what?" Fox said. "You
could be the queen of the birds!"
The proud crow nodded.

"You are pretty too!" said Fox.

"I like black feathers."

"Crr, crr," said Crow.

"You are welcome," said Fox.

"Sniff, sniff." Fox's nose led him to a tree. Crow was sitting on it.

"Hello, friend!" Fox said.

"Crr," said Crow. Her beak was stuffed with cheese. She could not say a word.

"You can really fly," said Fox.
"That was great."
"Crr, crr," said Crow.
"You are welcome," said Fox.

"You must have very strong wings," said Fox.
"Crr, crr," said Crow.
"You are welcome," said Fox.

© Scott Foresman 2

Scott Foresman
Reading

Grade 2
Phonics Reader 2

**When Hen Went
Shopping**
by Fay Robinson
illustrated by
Matt Straub

Phonics Skills:
• Short *e*, *o*
• Final consonant blends

Scott Foresman
**Phonics
System**

Scott Foresman

When Hen
Went Shopping

by Fay Robinson
illustrated by Matt Straub

This book belongs to

_____

Phonics for Families: This book contains words with the short vowels *e* and *o*, as in *hen* and *spot*, and final consonant blends. It also provides practice reading the high-frequency words *made*, *taste* and *your*. After reading the book with your child, search through the story together to find words with short *e* and short *o*.

Phonics Skill: Short *e*, *o*; Final consonant blends

High-Frequency Words: *made*, *taste*, *your*

Then Hen asked, "Now how do
I look?"

"Great!" said her friends. Hen
felt the same way.

"You see," she said, "shopping
was a good idea!"

When Hen Went Shopping

by Fay Robinson
illustrated by Matt Straub

Scott Foresman

Editorial Offices: Glenview, Illinois • New York, New York
Sales Offices: Reading, Massachusetts • Duluth, Georgia
Glenview, Illinois • Carrollton, Texas • Menlo Park, California

Hen was tired of how she looked. "Dog has spots. Cat has stripes. Fox has a red coat. And Frog is as green as the grass. I don't have spots or stripes. I don't even have a color. I just have plain old white feathers," said Hen.

© Scott Foresman 2

"And those things on your feet are for swimming. Hens can't swim. You don't need them," said Frog.
So Hen took off the things on her feet.

"And stripes look better on cats than on hens," said Cat. "You might look better without them."
So Hen took off the striped vest.

Hen jumped off her nest. She landed with a bump. "I want to change. I am going shopping!" she said.
She drew up a list.

Dog tried to stop her. "You look fine just the way you are. You have good taste," he said.

"Do not waste your time!" said Frog.

Hen had made up her mind. She went into town.

"And, if you ask me, a red coat is for a fox," said Fox.

So Hen took off the red coat.

"Well," said Dog, "spots are for dogs. You might look better without them."

So Hen took off the spotted scarf.

Hen found the store she was looking for.

"Oh! What a nice scarf!" Hen said. Then she found a striped vest! She held up a red coat. "Does this come in my size?" she asked.

"Your coat is very red," said Fox. "And the things on your feet are very green," said Frog.
"Yes," said Hen. "But what about ME? Don't I look great?"

"How do I look?" asked Hen.
Dog said, "Well, your scarf is
very spotted."

"And your vest has lots of stripes,"
said Cat.

Hen also found some green
things for her feet. "I'll get these. I'll
be just like Frog!" she said. "I will
look as good as everyone else!

"Now I am all done!" she said.
Then Hen ran home.

Hen went into her house. She
put on everything at once.

Hen stepped into the yard.
"Come see!" she called.
Her friends stood around her.
No one said a word.

Scott Foresman
Reading

Grade 2
Phonics Reader 3

**Check Out These
Animals!**
by Joan Cottle
illustrated by
Neecy Twinem

Phonics Skills:
- Long vowels with
  final *e*
- Initial consonant
  digraphs

Scott Foresman
**Phonics
System**

Scott Foresman

Check Out
These Animals!

by Joan Cottle
illustrated by Neecy Twinem

This book belongs to

_____

Phonics for Families: This book features words with long vowels with final *e*; words that begin with the letters *ch, sh, th,* and *wh;* and the high-frequency words *clean, use, work,* and *world.* Read the book together. Then ask your child to talk about the animal fact he or she likes best.

Phonics Skills: Long vowels with final *e;* Initial consonant digraphs

High-Frequency Words: *clean, use, work, world*

No way! But many ducks make long trips. A duck can fly 900 miles in a day.

Check Out These Animals!

by Joan Cottle
illustrated by Neecy Twinem

Scott Foresman

Editorial Offices: Glenview, Illinois • New York, New York
Sales Offices: Reading, Massachusetts • Duluth, Georgia
Glenview, Illinois • Carrollton, Texas • Menlo Park, California

These animals are great! Just
check out these animal facts.
You will think so too.

Do ducks run away from home?

No. But male moose do work
hard. They carry around big
antlers. Some moose carry 70
pounds of antlers! That must be
hard work!

Why don't sharks need a dentist?

A great white shark has
many teeth. If a tooth falls out,
a sharp, clean new one takes
its place.

4

Does a moose go to work?

13

No one knows! But we do know they can sleep a long time! On sunny days, snails use their shells for shade. They just go inside. A snail can sleep for three or four years.

How big is a cow?

A cow can tip the scale at more than 900 pounds. In one day, a cow might chew 80 pounds of food. It can drink 40 gallons of water.

Do snails dream?

You bet! A baby blue whale drinks more than 100 gallons of milk a day. In a few seconds, it can drink gallons of milk.

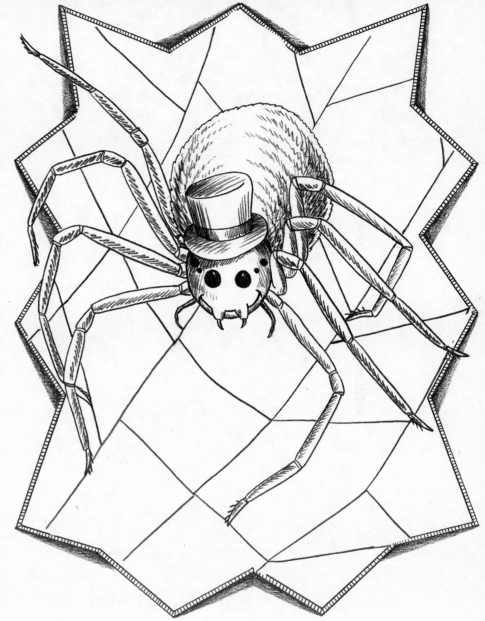

How big was the biggest spider web in the world?

The biggest web was 20 feet from side to side. That is as wide as four cars!

8

Does a baby whale get thirsty?

9

Grade 2
Phonics Reader 4

**Sweet Pea,
the Black Sheep**
by Stacey Sparks
illustrated by
Lisa Zolnowski

Phonics Skills:
• Long e spelled *ea, ee*
• Final consonant digraphs

Scott Foresman

Sweet Pea, the Black Sheep

by Stacey Sparks
illustrated by Lisa Zolnowski

This book belongs to

_____

Phonics for Families: This book will give your child practice in reading words with the long *e* sound spelled *ee* and *ea*, words that end with the letters *ch*, *ng*, *nk*, *sh*, *tch*, and *th*, and the high-frequency words *should*, *would*, *their*, *through*, and *very*. Read the book together with your child. Then see how many words with long *e* your child can find.

Phonics Skills: Long *e* spelled *ea*, *ee*; Final consonant digraphs

High-Frequency Words: *should*, *would*, *their*, *through*, *very*

Sweet Pea feels cool now. That is good. Soon it will be summer. Then fall will come, followed by winter and spring. And another year will pass on the farm.

Sweet Pea, the Black Sheep

by Stacey Sparks
illustrated by Lisa Zolnowski

Scott Foresman

Editorial Offices: Glenview, Illinois • New York, New York
Sales Offices: Reading, Massachusetts • Duluth, Georgia
Glenview, Illinois • Carrollton, Texas • Menlo Park, California

It is spring on the farm. This lamb was just born.

At first the lamb is very weak. The mother sheep stays with her lamb. Soon the lamb will get up.

It is spring again. It is the time for more lambs. It is also time to cut Sweet Pea's fleece. The farmer gets a big batch to sell. It will be made into cloth. The farmer must keep the fleece clean. Clean wool is worth more.

The farmer must check Sweet Pea's feet. They look fine. They are nice and long.

The lamb says, "Baaa." The mother bleats back. Now they know each other. If the lamb gets lost, it will bleat. The bleat will lead the mother to the lamb.

The farmer names this new lamb Sweet Pea.

Now Sweet Pea is three days old. She can leave the pen. She goes out with the rest of the flock. The mother stays close to watch. She will keep Sweet Pea safe.

4

The snow is thick. The sheep cannot reach the grass through it. They need something to eat. The farmer must bring hay for their meal.

13

Winter is here. Before they go to sleep, the kids wish for snow. They get their wish. They rush out to play.

But the farmer does not seem happy. Why would the farmer be sad?

Sweet Pea is getting big. She plays with other lambs. They run through the field. They run up a pile of hay. Then they fall in a heap!

It is summer. The sheep are eating grass and weeds. Sheep are easy to feed. Weeds and grass are cheap!

The farmer has made a shed. Sweet Pea can go to the shed to get out of the heat.

She should be the very best sheep at the fair!

The farmer is smiling. Sweet Pea is a good sheep. She is strong. She is clean. She is pretty.

The farmer will teach Sweet Pea a trick. He calls her name. Then he holds out a treat. The treat is a peanut. Sweet Pea comes. Then she gets the snack. Soon Sweet Pea should come when she is called.

Sweet Pea sticks out her neck.
What does this mean? Do you
think she wants more peanuts?
No. This means, "Would you
scratch my chin?"

8

It is fall. Sweet Pea's wool is
getting thick and long. The farmer
gives Sweet Pea a bath. She is
going to the fair!

9

Scott Foresman
Reading

Grade 2
Phonics Reader 5

The Oldest Car in Merry County
by Lucy Floyd
illustrated by
Suzette Barbier

Phonics Skills:
• Long e spelled *e, y*
• Inflected ending *ed*
  (without spelling change)

Scott Foresman
Phonics System

Scott Foresman

The Oldest Car in Merry County

by Lucy Floyd
illustrated by Suzette Barbier

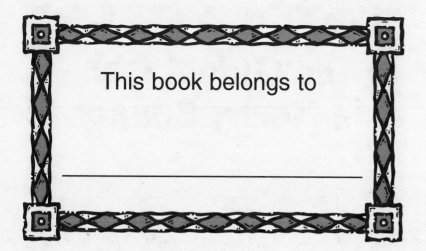

This book belongs to

_____

Phonics for Families: This book provides practice in reading words with the long *e* sound spelled *e* and *y* and words with the *ed* ending. It also provides practice reading the high-frequency words *these, off, took, house,* and *never*. Read the book with your child. Then invite him or her to design an advertisement for the Old Car Museum.

Phonics Skills: Long *e* spelled *e, y;* Inflected ending *-ed* (without spelling change)

High-Frequency Words: *these, off, took, house, never*

Now kids from all over Merry County come to see Polly.

She is the oldest and only car in the Old Car Museum!

16

The Oldest Car in Merry County

by Lucy Floyd
illustrated by Suzette Barbier

Scott Foresman

Editorial Offices: Glenview, Illinois • New York, New York
Sales Offices: Reading, Massachusetts • Duluth, Georgia
Glenview, Illinois • Carrollton, Texas • Menlo Park, California

Mrs. Dotty had a very, very
old car she called Polly. Polly
was the oldest car in Merry
County. Maybe it was the oldest
car anywhere.

"We are going to miss Polly!"
said Billy.

"What can we do?" asked Sally.

"Hmm," said Billy.

They talked and talked. Then
they had an idea!

"Get Polly into the garage,"
said Willy.
Everyone helped push Polly
into Mrs. Dotty's garage.

Mrs. Dotty washed and waxed
Polly every day.
"Polly, you look pretty," said
Mrs. Dotty. "And all these kids
like you."

"Off we go, Polly!" yelled Mrs.
Dotty as she took a spin around
the block. She had to yell because
Polly was very noisy.

Polly went, "Clacky-clack-clack."

"Way to go!" yelled Mrs. Dotty.

"Maybe," said Mrs. Dotty. "But
I will never be happy without
Polly. And these kids will miss
Polly too."

Willy looked under the hood.
He pushed and pulled. He
pounded and shouted.

"Polly is very old," he said. "I
can't fix Polly. Do you want me
to tow Polly away?"

Mrs. Dotty drove by Sally's house.
"Hello, Polly!" called Sally.
Polly went, "Clacky-clack-clack."
"Way to go!" called Mrs. Dotty.
And off she went.

Mrs. Dotty took the car by
Billy's house.
"Hello, Polly!" called Billy.
Polly went, "Clacky-clack-clack."
"Way to go!" yelled Mrs. Dotty.
And off she went.

"What happened?" asked Billy.
"Is Polly broken?" asked Sally.
"Maybe," said Mrs. Dotty.
Just then Polly made a funny
sound again.

"I'll call Willy," said Mrs. Dotty. "He will fix Polly."

Mrs. Dotty was almost home. Then Polly made a funny sound. "What's that?" asked Mrs. Dotty. "Polly has never done that before."

Polly made another funny sound.
"What's going on?" asked
Mrs. Dotty.

Polly slowed down. Then Polly
would not move at all.

8

Mrs. Dotty took a look under
the hood. She pushed and pulled.
She pounded and shouted. But
Polly would not move.

© Scott Foresman 2

9

Scott Foresman Reading

Grade 2
Phonics Reader 6

Quail for Dinner
by Maryann Dobeck
illustrated by
Joe Boddy

Phonics Skills:
• Long *a* spelled *a, ai, ay*
• Inflected endings
  -es, -ing, -s (without
  spelling change)

Scott Foresman
Phonics System

Scott Foresman

Quail for Dinner

by Maryann Dobeck
illustrated by Joe Boddy

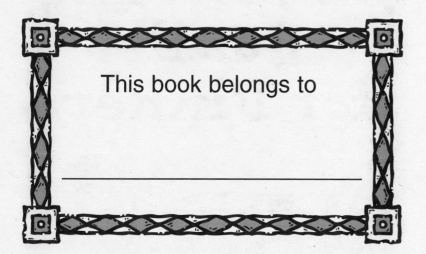

This book belongs to

_____

Phonics for Families: This book features words with the long *a* sound, such as *apron*, *quail*, and *way*, and words with endings *-ing*, *-s*, and *-es*. It also provides practice reading the words *mother*, *new*, *warm*, *keep*, and *myself*. Encourage your child to make a sign that uses some of these words.

Phonics Skills: Long *a* spelled *a*, *ai*, *ay*; Inflected endings *-es*, *-ing*, *-s* (without spelling change)

High-Frequency Words: *mother*, *new*, *warm*, *keep*, *myself*

"Hello, Quail," says the King. "Join us for dinner. We will have rice and beans. Bring all your animal friends."

"Hooray!" yells Quail. "Hail to the King!"

16

Quail for Dinner

by Maryann Dobeck
illustrated by Joe Boddy

Scott Foresman

Editorial Offices: Glenview, Illinois • New York, New York
Sales Offices: Reading, Massachusetts • Duluth, Georgia
Glenview, Illinois • Carrollton, Texas • Menlo Park, California

"I want something new for dinner," says the King. "How about quail?"

"Rice and beans!" squeals Pig.
"Hooray!" snorts Horse.
"Hooray!" shouts Sheep.
"I will go find Quail," says Pig.
"I will go warm our dinner," says Cook.

"Well, well," says the King.
"Quail misses me! Find her.
Then we will invite her to eat
dinner with us."

"What shall we eat?" asks
the cook.

"We can eat rice and beans,"
says the King.

"Fine," says the cook. And she
puts on her apron.

"Oh, no!" says Quail. "The King wants quail for dinner. I am in danger. I cannot stay here. I will have to run away by myself!"

Sheep gives the King a note. It says:
I have gone away by myself.
I miss you and all my friends.
Quail

On their way home, the King
and the cook read the new sign.
Then the King asks, "Have you
seen Quail?"

"She went away," says Horse.

On her way, Quail meets
Horse. He is pulling a cart.
"Where are you going?" asks Horse.

"Far, far away," says Quail.
"The King wants quail for dinner.
And the King always gets what
he wants."

On her way, Quail meets
Sheep. She is eating grass. "Why
are you rushing?" asks Sheep.
  "The King wants quail for
dinner. And the King always
gets what he wants," says Quail.

6

Horse puts up a sign too.
It says:
  Quail is a great mother.
  She watches her chicks.
  She keeps them safe.

11

The King and the cook are looking for Quail. As they pass the barn, they stop to read the new sign. Then the King asks, "Where is Quail?"

"I don't know," says Pig.

On her way, Quail meets Pig. He is rolling in mud. "What are you doing?" asks Pig.

"I am going away," says Quail. "The King wants quail for dinner. And the King always gets what he wants."

Pig says, "Just keep going. I have a plan. We will find you later."
"Okay," says Quail.

Quail is a great mother.
She keeps her eggs warm.
She sits on them.
She sits until each one hatches.

Pig makes a sign. He puts it on the barn. It says:
Quail is a great mother.
She keeps her eggs warm.
She sits on them.
She sits until each one hatches.

Scott Foresman
Reading

Grade 2
Phonics Reader 7

Fly High!
by Lee S. Justice
illustrated by
Robert Lawson

Phonics Skills:
- Long *i* spelled *i, igh, y*
- Medial consonants
  (including double
  medial consonants)

Scott Foresman
Phonics System

Scott Foresman

Fly High!

by Lee S. Justice
illustrated by Robert Lawson

This book belongs to

_____

Phonics for Families: This book gives your child practice with the long *i* sound spelled *i, igh,* and *y;* words with a consonant in the middle such as *before, never,* and *pilot;* and the high-frequency words *because, carry,* and *whole.* Ask your child to read the book aloud. Then take turns finding words that contain the long *i* sound.

Phonics Skill: Long *i* spelled *i, igh, y;* Medial consonants (including double medial consonants)

High-Frequency Words: *because, carry, whole*

A few years went by. Because the brothers' machine worked, more people made flying machines. More pilots tried to fly high.

One day, Orville invited his father on a flight. Father had never seen the sky so close before. He called out, "Higher, Orville! Higher!"

Fly High!

by Lee S. Justice
illustrated by Robert Lawson

Scott Foresman

Editorial Offices: Glenview, Illinois • New York, New York
Sales Offices: Reading, Massachusetts • Duluth, Georgia
Glenview, Illinois • Carrollton, Texas • Menlo Park, California

When they were children, Wilbur and Orville never thought that they might fly an airplane.

In 1878, there were no airplanes and no cars. But one day Father gave them a present. The present made them think about flying.

At Kitty Hawk, Wilbur tried the Flyer first. It did not stay up. Then Orville was the pilot. The Flyer lifted off. It flew! The flight lasted 12 whole seconds!

The Wright brothers had made the world's first flying machine.

A glider needs wind to fly. But a real flying machine would not need wind. Its power would come from a motor.

Then Wilbur and Orville made plans for a flying machine with a motor. They called it the Flyer.

The present was a toy that would fly up high in the air. They called it the Bat. They tried to make the Bat fly high into the sky.

When the Bat broke, the
brothers fixed it. Mother made
toys for her children. She also
fixed them when they broke.

But they tried again. They made
a machine to blow wind. They
tested all kinds of wing shapes in
the wind. Then the brothers made
plans for a new glider.

Back at Kitty Hawk, this glider
could fly high!

The brothers made a new glider to bring to Kitty Hawk. The glider lifted off the beach. But it didn't fly high or far. It could not turn. Something was not right. The brothers felt like giving up.

Wilbur and Orville drew plans for toys. It was fun to think up ideas. It was fun to plan and build things.

Orville and Wilbur grew up. In their free time, they liked to ride bikes!

The brothers made a glider. Then they went to a place called Kitty Hawk. They tested their glider on the beach. It lifted off! It glided over the sand. Wilbur and Orville were pleased.

A kite that can carry a person
is called a glider. The Wright
brothers knew about a man who
had made gliders. The gliders
sometimes crashed because
they were hard to steer.

The brothers wanted to build
a glider that a pilot could steer.

Everyone was riding bikes.
New bikes were made better
than the old ones. A ride down
a hill felt like flying!

When a bike broke, help was
close by. The whole town knew
that the Wright brothers could
fix anything.

Wilbur and Orville opened a shop to fix bikes. Soon after that, they built bikes and sold them.

Then the brothers had an idea for a whole new machine.

Birds and bugs could fly. People could not. But maybe people could fly if they were in a machine.

Could Wilbur and Orville build a flying machine?

Grade 2
Phonics Reader 8

The Pond
by Anastasia Suen
illustrated by
Roger Chandler

Phonics Skills:
- *R*-controlled vowels
  (*er, ir, ur*)
- Plurals *-s* and *-es*
  (including changing *y*
  to *i* before adding *-es*)

Scott Foresman

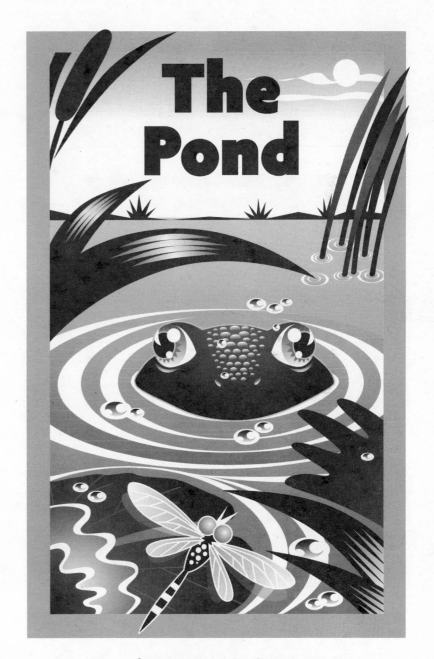

by Anastasia Suen
illustrated by Roger Chandler

This book belongs to

_____

Phonics for Families: This book features words that contain the vowel sounds heard in *perch, bird,* and *turtle,* plural words formed by adding *-s* and *-es,* and the high-frequency words *almost, another around, under,* and *food.* Invite your child to read the book aloud. Then have him/her talk about the animals and plants that he/she sees in your neighborhood.

Phonics Skills: *R*-controlled vowels (*er, ir, ur*); Plurals *-s* and *-es* (including changing *y* to *i* before adding *-es*)

High-Frequency Words: *almost, another, around, food, under*

A pond is a great place to visit. There is always something to see!

The Pond

by Anastasia Suen
illustrated by Roger Chandler

Scott Foresman

Editorial Offices: Glenview, Illinois • New York, New York
Sales Offices: Reading, Massachusetts • Duluth, Georgia
Glenview, Illinois • Carrollton, Texas • Menlo Park, California

All kinds of animals live
around a pond. Some animals
live in the water. Some animals
live near the water. Some animals
live in another place. But they
turn to the pond for food.

© Scott Foresman 2

If you come to the pond at
night, you can see wings. Bats
wake up at night and come out
to eat. They whirl and twirl over
the pond. They eat every insect
they can find!

Water striders are bugs that
walk on top of the water. How
do they do it? They are very
light. Also, their feet help them
float. Water striders eat other
insects.

Plants live in a pond too.
Fat lily pads float on the water.
Water lilies turn to the sun.
Weeds float in another spot.
Reeds stand tall in the water.

At first, fish eggs float in the water until they hatch. The fish babies hide under lily pads and other plants in the pond. Small fish swim in a school to stay safe.

If you want to see painted turtles, you must be very quiet. These small turtles slide into the water when they hear any sound. Painted turtles eat water plants and insects.

Watch out for snapping turtles! Snappers move quickly. They have very sharp jaws. Snapping turtles eat fish, birds, and other turtles!

Big fish try to hide too. This perch is hard to see. It is dark on the top. It is shiny on the bottom. If you look down at the perch, it looks like the water. If you look up at the perch, its shiny scales look like the sky.

Catfish spend their time near the dirt at the bottom of the pond. They look as if they have horns near their mouth. Catfish do not have scales like the perch.

Garter snakes come to the pond to find food. They eat frogs, toads, and worms. Garter snakes have stripes on their backs.

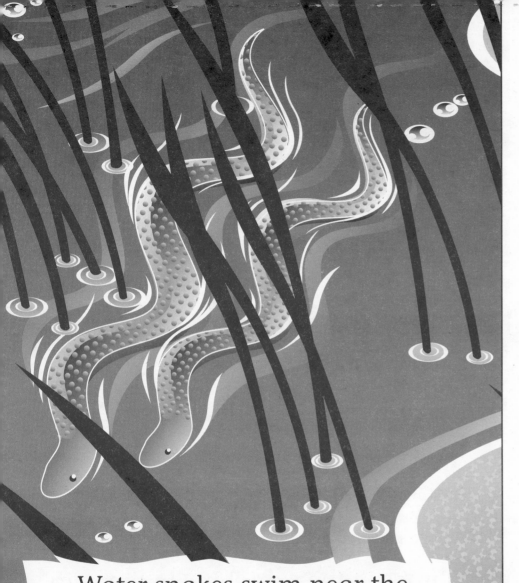

Water snakes swim near the top of the water. Or they swim deep under the water. They find their food in the pond.

Some ducks turn upside down to eat. Do you see their tails in the air? Other ducks swim under the water to find food. All ducks eat plants and insects.

Tadpoles grow inside eggs. Little tadpoles almost look like fish. Soon these tadpoles will grow legs. Then you can see that they are frogs.

A bullfrog is one of the biggest frogs in the world! It can grow up to eight inches long. Bullfrogs eat almost anything smaller than they are.

Scott Foresman
Reading

Grade 2
Phonics Reader 9

**A Day in the Life
of a Firefighter**
by Lucy Floyd
illustrated by
Donald Cook

Phonics Skills:
• Long *o* spelled *o, oa,
  ow, oe*
• Compound words

Scott Foresman
Phonics System

Scott Foresman

A Day in the Life
of a Firefighter

by Lucy Floyd
illustrated by Donald Cook

This book belongs to

_____

© Scott Foresman 2

Phonics for Families: This book provides practice reading compound words such as *firefighters* and *outside* and words with the long vowel *o* sound spelled *o, oa, ow,* and *oe*. It also includes the high-frequency words *animals, before, between, knew,* and *why*. Read the book with your child. Then go back through the book and have your child find words with the long vowel *o* sound.

Phonics Skills: Long *o* spelled *o, oa, ow, oe;* Compound words

High-Frequency Words: *animals, before, between, knew, why*

"This was not a slow day!"
Joe says.

"No," Maria says. "We don't
get so many slow days. But I
like my job!"

16

A Day in the Life of a Firefighter

by Lucy Floyd
illustrated by Donald Cook

Scott Foresman

Editorial Offices: Glenview, Illinois • New York, New York
Sales Offices: Reading, Massachusetts • Duluth, Georgia
Glenview, Illinois • Carrollton, Texas • Menlo Park, California

It is only six o'clock in the morning. Most people are sleeping. But a bright red truck races down the road. Maria Lopez is on the truck.

It is six o'clock. Maria is near the doorway. Her day is over and she is ready to go home. Joe talks to her before she goes.

"There was a fire at the airport," Joe says. "The airport firefighters put it out themselves. They used foam to put it out."

Maria shows everyone what firefighters wear. She says that the special clothes keep them safe. She shows them the air tank they hold on their backs.

Maria is a firefighter. Her job is to save people and put out fires. Today, she and the other firefighters are going to a fire on Poe Road.

Maria is on a ladder truck. This truck holds ladders that can reach anyone in a tall building. The other truck has a pump and hoses.

She tells the kids that things should not be left close to stoves. Most of all, homes should have smoke alarms.

It is two o'clock in the afternoon. Maria is in a school. She is talking about fires.

"Everyone must know the way out in case of a fire," Maria says.

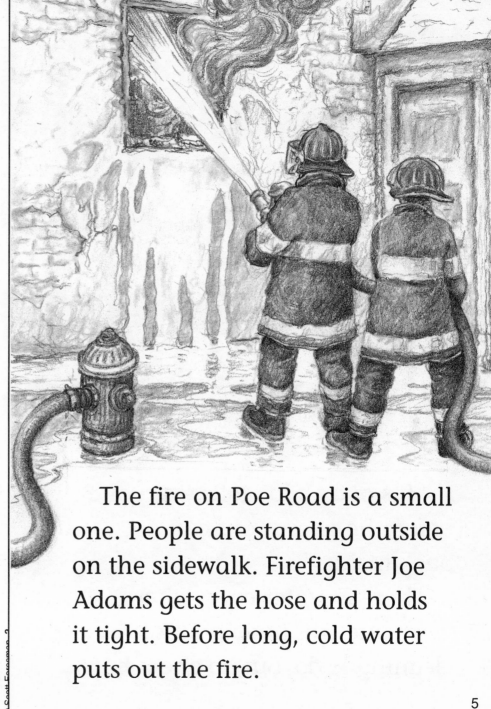

The fire on Poe Road is a small one. People are standing outside on the sidewalk. Firefighter Joe Adams gets the hose and holds it tight. Before long, cold water puts out the fire.

"It's okay," Joe tells everyone before he goes. "You can go back inside."

There is water everywhere. Everyone will have a lot of cleaning to do. But no one is hurt.

Maria is good with animals. She reaches for the cat. She holds it in her hands. "You will be warm inside," Maria says. The cat is okay.

A long ladder takes Maria up to the roof. She walks over to the cat.

"Hello," she says in a low voice. "You must be cold."

Joe and Maria are back at the firehouse. They are in between calls. Joe asks, "When did you know you wanted to be a firefighter?"

"I knew before I was seven years old," Maria tells Joe. "Do you want to know why?"

"Yes," says Joe. "Go on."

"My own dog was trapped in a building that was on fire," Maria says. "He was stuck between the wall and the bed. We couldn't get him out. But the firefighters saved him before he was hurt. That was when I knew I wanted to be a firefighter. I knew I wanted to save people and animals too."

It is ten o'clock. Maria races downtown on the firetruck. Why are the firefighters called this time? A cat is sitting on a chimney. The top of the chimney is open. The man who owns the cat is in the backyard. He is scared that the cat will fall in the chimney.

Grade 2
Phonics Reader 10

**The Town Mouse and
the Country Mouse**
retold by Judy Nayer
illustrated by
Marvin Glass

Phonics Skills:
• Words with *ce, ge, se*
• Possessives (singular
  and plural)

The Town Mouse and
the Country Mouse

retold by Judy Nayer
illustrated by Marvin Glass

This book belongs to

_____

Phonics for Families: This book provides practice reading words with the letters *ce, ge,* and *se,* as in *mice, huge, house,* and *cheese;* words that show possession, such as *hens'* and *friend's;* and the high-frequency words *enough, full, heard,* and *until.* Read the book together. Then have your child find words in the book that show things belong to someone.

Phonics Skills: Words with *ce, ge, se;* Possessives (singular and plural)

High-Frequency Words: *enough, full, heard, until*

"You can keep your huge feast," said the Country Mouse. "I'll stick to eating bits of cheese at my place. Even a cage would be better than here! At least I could eat cheese in peace."

And so the Country Mouse went home. She went home to her happy little house.

16

The Town Mouse and the Country Mouse

retold by Judy Nayer
illustrated by Marvin Glass

Scott Foresman

Editorial Offices: Glenview, Illinois • New York, New York
Sales Offices: Reading, Massachusetts • Duluth, Georgia
Glenview, Illinois • Carrollton, Texas • Menlo Park, California

Once there was a Country Mouse. She made her home inside a barn. She ate the hens' wheat and the pigs' feed. And sometimes she found bits of the farmer's cheese to eat.

The little mouse was happy in her house. "What a nice place!" she said.

"Good-by?" said her friend.

"Yes, you heard me. I am going home. I do not want to see that cat twice."

"But there is still more to eat," said the Town Mouse.

"It's all right," said the Town Mouse. "It is the people's cat. We'll just wait until he goes. Then we'll go back for more."

"No, thank you," said the Country Mouse. "I've had enough. Good-by, my friend."

One day the Country Mouse's friend came to visit. He was a Town Mouse.

"How nice to see you!" said the Country Mouse. "Let me show you around my place."

The Country Mouse showed her
friend around. Then she gave him
the best bits of cheese she had.

The Town Mouse ate the cheese
bits at once. "These are good," he
said. "Do you have anything else?"

Then she saw a huge cat. It
was about to pounce on the table!
The two mice ran down the side
of the table and found a safe
place to hide.

They were almost full when they heard a hiss.

"What was that?" asked the Country Mouse.

"No," said the Country Mouse. "But I can go outside and look for something else."

"That's all right," the Town Mouse said. "I've had enough. I must be going anyway."

© Scott Foresman 2

The Town Mouse got up to go. Then he said, "Why don't you come with me? There is a lot to eat at my house!"

The two mice ran onto the table and began to eat.
"You were right!" Country Mouse said. "You live like a prince here!"

Inside was a huge table with lace on top of it. The Country Mouse's face lit up. The table was full of food! The cheese was as large as she was!

The Country Mouse had heard about life in town. "I don't know," she said. "I like my place."

"Please," said the Town Mouse. "You will like my place too."

She didn't want to hurt her friend's feelings. So off they went.

Soon enough they were at the Town Mouse's place. The Country Mouse had never seen anything like it. The house was huge! It looked like a king's palace!

"I thought my place was nice," she said. "Until I saw this!"
The Town Mouse took his friend inside.

©Scott Foresman 2

Scott Foresman Reading

Grade 2
Phonics Reader 11

**Out and About
on the *Mayflower***
by Judy Veramendi
illustrated by
David Wenzel

Phonics Skills:
• Vowel diphthongs
  ou, ow
• Inflected endings
  (doubling final
  consonants before
  -ed, -ing)

Scott Foresman

Out and About on the *Mayflower*

by Judy Veramendi
illustrated by David Wenzel

This book belongs to

_____

Phonics for Families: This book features words with the sound heard in *cloud* and *brown*, and action words in which the final letter was doubled before *-ed* or *-ing* was added. It also provides practice reading the high-frequency words *been, friend, since, show,* and *those*. Read the book aloud with your child. Then ask him or her to tell how Grace might have felt on the ship.

Phonics Skills: Vowel diphthongs *ou, ow;* Inflected endings (doubling final consonants before *-ed, -ing*)

High-Frequency Words: *been, friend, show, since, those*

Then I spotted it too!
Soon people started running
around the deck. Everyone was
hugging each other.
We had found our new home!

16

Out and About on the *Mayflower*

by Judy Veramendi
illustrated by David Wenzel

Scott Foresman

Editorial Offices: Glenview, Illinois • New York, New York
Sales Offices: Reading, Massachusetts • Duluth, Georgia
Glenview, Illinois • Carrollton, Texas • Menlo Park, California

September 16, 1620

We are about to leave our home and our friends. We are setting sail on the *Mayflower*. We must find a new land.

My friend Hope cannot come with us. The ship is too crowded.

2

November 21, 1620

The lookout woke us up. He shouted, "Land-ho!"

I rubbed my eyes. I rushed out on the deck. "Where's the land?" I asked.

"See that long brown line under those clouds?" he shouted. "That is land!"

15

November 16, 1620

Now the water is running out! People are getting sick too.

It has been two months since we left home. When will we see land?

Hope is sobbing. So am I. She has been my best friend since I was small.

September 23, 1620

We have been at sea for one week now. Dolphins are swimming near us. Today I counted six. Those dolphins are my new friends.

© Scott Foresman 2

Faith's mother came to show us the baby. He's so sweet! We are going to play with him as soon as we are allowed!

November 1, 1620
    Today Faith's mom had a baby.
Now Faith has a new little brother.
    Yes, a baby was born on the
Mayflower!

    One dolphin seemed to be calling
out to me. It made loud clacking
sounds. I think it grinned too!

September 26, 1620

My little brother likes getting around the ship. Today Goodman has been running around and around the deck. He keeps getting in the sailors' way. They keep telling him to get out of the way.

We just heard a loud sound. One of the sailors is yelling for help. The mast is splitting!

The sailors are propping up the mast. It seems okay for now.

October 15, 1620

    Waves as high as houses have been hitting us for days. We have been sitting below deck. It's so crowded.

    The ship is bouncing up and down. The wind is howling!

September 29, 1620

    Clouds and sea, clouds and sea. That is all I see when I look out.

    One of the sailors said there are thirty-two children on the ship. I am glad that some of those children are my friends.

September 30, 1620

It has been two weeks since we left home. The good food is running out. Now all we have to eat is hardtack. It is a hard, dry cracker. How I wish for good food!

There is one good thing about this bad food. It helped me to get to know my friend Faith.

Yesterday Faith was groaning about the hardtack. I was too! We grinned at each other.

Now we are about to go up on the deck. Maybe we can spend time spotting dolphins. I hope to show her my new friends.

Scott Foresman
Reading

Grade 2
Phonics Reader 12

Just Start
by Maryann Dobeck
illustrated by
Eva Vagretti Cockrille

Phonics Skills:
- *R*-controlled vowel *ar*
- Inflected endings
  (dropping *e* before
  -ed, *-ing*)

Scott Foresman
Phonics System

Scott Foresman

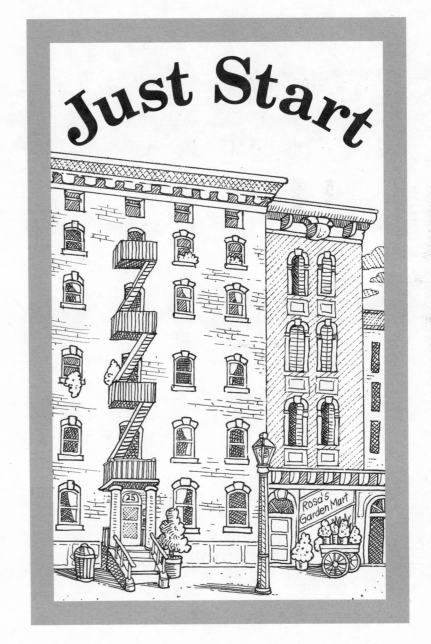

Just Start

by Maryann Dobeck
illustrated by Eva Vagretti Cockrille

This book belongs to

_____

Phonics for Families: This book features words with the vowel sound heard in *farm* and *start*; and words that have the endings *-ed* and *-ing*, as in *liked* and *waving*. It also provides practice reading the high-frequency words *children*, *city*, *high*, *place*, and *room*. After reading the book together, encourage your child to talk about something he or she enjoyed doing for someone else.

Phonics Skill: *R*-controlled vowel *ar;* Inflected endings (dropping *e* before *-ed, -ing*)

Featured High-Frequency Words: *children, city, high, place, room*

"Happy Birthday, Grandma!"
I said. "I planted these for you."

"Oh, Honey Bun!" said
Grandma. "I have a garden
again." Then she added, "But
wasn't it hard to do all this?"

"Nothing is too hard to try," I
said. "You just have to start!"

16

Just Start

by Maryann Dobeck
illustrated by Eva Vagretti Cockrille

Scott Foresman

Editorial Offices: Glenview, Illinois • New York, New York
Sales Offices: Reading, Massachusetts • Duluth, Georgia
Glenview, Illinois • Carrollton, Texas • Menlo Park, California

I live on a farm. My Grandma lives in the city. Her apartment building is six stories high. She lives on the first floor.

Grandma invited me to visit her in the city. I stayed for part of the summer.

Everyone came to Grandma's birthday party. She loved her gifts. Mom gave her a scarf.

I took Grandma's arm. "My gift is in the yard," I said. "Come outside."

Rosa's Garden Mart was down the street. Other children joined me as I ran. I arrived at Rosa's. There was a cart full of flowers in front.

"Can you help me?" I asked her. "I have five dollars."

My friends helped me carry everything home.

So, when school ended, Mom drove me to Grandma's.

Grandma was waving and smiling as we parked the car. "Come here, Honey Bun!" she called, as I got out of the car. "How big you are!"

My name is Shamara. But
Grandma calls me Honey Bun.
That is because I like the sweet
rolls she is always baking.

After Mom left, I went to my
room. On the bed was a city
map. There was a red mark
next to each fun place to visit.

I ran to my room and got my
paints. I started making a large
sign. Then I took the money I
had saved in a jar. I raced
through the yard.

At the market, Mr. March
found two large wooden boxes
in the back room.

"I've got to get started," I said.

"I'm making apple tarts for
the party," said Mrs. Hardy.

Mr. March said he would start
baking a large cake.

We started out early the next
day, riding the subway to the
Art in the Park show. One artist
was carving a duck.

"That must be hard to do,"
I said.

"Nothing is too hard to try,"
said Grandma. "You just have
to start."

Grandma took me everywhere in the city. We liked going from place to place. The buildings were so high!

I told Mrs. Hardy my plan for Grandma's birthday party.

"Great!" said Mrs. Hardy. "I'd like to take part too! First, let's talk to Mr. March at the market. Maybe he can find some better boxes for you."

I started to plan a party for Grandma's birthday. I remember seeing two boxes in the backyard. I raced outside and found two large boxes.

"What are you doing with those boxes?" asked Mrs. Hardy. She was taking her dog to the park.

It was not hard to find children to play with. We had fun skating in the park. We played in Grandma's small yard. On hot days, we liked taking a swim in the city pool.

Summer in the city was perfect!

But when Mom's note came, I started to miss the farm. My garden was in bloom. Mom sent a picture of all the flowers I had planted in the spring.

"Did you ever have a garden?" I asked Grandma.

"Yes, I did," she said. "Grandpa and I used to win first place for our roses. They were dark, dark red. That was a long time ago!"

Scott Foresman
Reading

Grade 2
Phonics Reader 13

**Have You Seen the
New Newts?**
by Meish Goldish
illustrated by BB Sams

Phonics Skills:
- Vowel patterns
  ew, oo, ou
- Contractions

Scott Foresman
Phonics System

Scott Foresman

Have You Seen the New Newts?

by Meish Goldish
illustrated by BB Sams

This book belongs to

_____

Phonics for Families: This book gives your child practice reading contractions and words that contain the vowel sound heard in *new, goose,* and *you.* It also features the high-frequency words *across, best, either, toward,* and *sometimes.* Read the book with your child. Then invite your child to name other animals whose names contain the *ew, oo,* and *ou* sounds.

Phonics Skills: Vowel patterns *ew, oo, ou;* Contractions

High-Frequency Words: *across, best, either, toward, sometimes*

"The boots are cool!" said the new newts. "They're a cool home!"

Goose scooped up the new newts and flew them to the pool.

"If you want to be cool, stay in the pool!" Goose said.

And so they did!

16

Have You Seen the New Newts?

by Meish Goldish
illustrated by BB Sams

Scott Foresman

Editorial Offices: Glenview, Illinois • New York, New York
Sales Offices: Reading, Massachusetts • Duluth, Georgia
Glenview, Illinois • Carrollton, Texas • Menlo Park, California

It was late afternoon at the zoo. Goose was trying to find the new newts. She saw Loon in the pool. Loon was swooping down in the water and scooping up fish.

Just then, one of the newts came up from inside the boot. Then the other newt came up from inside the other boot!

"What are you doing in there?" asked Kangaroo. "You've got everyone in the zoo trying to find you!"

Kangaroo sat down to put on his boots. He knew they'd help him hop across the zoo.

Kangaroo felt something move inside one boot.

"Shoo, shoo!" said Kangaroo.

Goose flew toward Loon. "Yoo-hoo, Loon!" called Goose. "Have you seen the new newts?"

"No," said Loon. "Sometimes they're here in the pool. But I haven't seen either one all day."

Next, Goose flew to Rooster on the roof.

"Yoo-hoo, Rooster!" called Goose. "Have you seen the new newts?"

Just then, Kangaroo came by. "What's going on?" he asked.

"We're going to try and find the new newts," Goose said.

"I'd like to help too," said Kangaroo. "I'll just put on my boots first."

Soon, other zoo animals grouped together to help find the new newts. In the group were Goose, Loon, Rooster, Raccoon, Poodle, Toucan, and Cuckoo.

"No," said Rooster. "I've been on the roof all day. They've not come up here." Then Rooster asked, "Want some noodle soup?"

"No, thank you," said Goose.

"Cock-a-noodle-noo!" said Rooster.

Goose then flew across the yard toward Raccoon. As always, Raccoon was snooping through the zoo for food.

"Yoo-hoo, Raccoon!" said Goose. "Have you seen the new newts?"

"We've not seen either of them all day," said Toucan.

"Are you sure?" Goose asked.

"We're sure," Cuckoo said. "But we'd be glad to help you find them."

"Great!" said Goose.

Goose said to herself, "Where's the best place to go next?" Then she saw Toucan and Cuckoo in a tree. Goose flew toward them.

"Have you seen the new newts?" Goose asked.

"I'd like to say yes," said Raccoon. "But I've got to say no. I haven't seen either one of them."

Then Raccoon saw an old soup can and began singing, "I'm in the mood for food."

Goose flew across the zoo. Poodle was cooling off outside her room.

"Yoo-hoo, Poodle!" said Goose. "Have you seen the new newts?"

8

"You'd better not ask me," said Poodle. "I've been in my room all afternoon getting a shampoo. Do you like my new hairdo?"

"Yes," said Goose. "Now you've got loops that don't droop!"

9

Scott Foresman
Reading

Grade 2
Phonics Reader 14

Orlando
by Nat Gabriel
illustrated by
Mike Reed

Phonics Skills:
- *R*-controlled vowels
  (*or, ore, oor, our*)
- Inflected endings
  (changing *y* to *i* before
  -ed, -es)

Scott Foresman
Phonics System

Scott Foresman

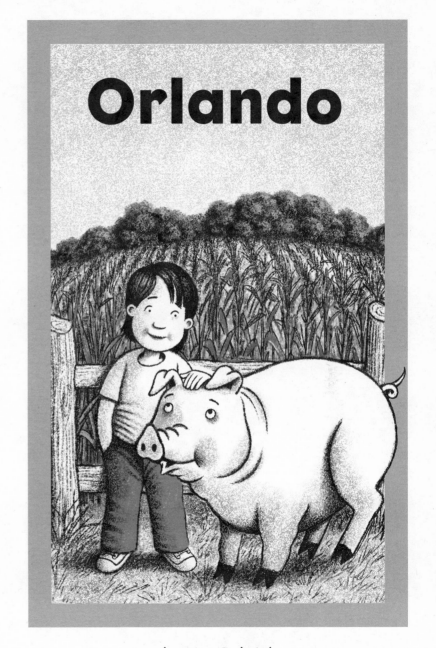

Orlando

by Nat Gabriel
illustrated by Mike Reed

This book belongs to

_____

"Orlando saved me," Salvador said.

"Yes, I know," said Mama. "He is family! We will just have to find room for him at our next place."

This brought a smile to Salvador's face. Orlando was saved!

"Now he really is a member of our family!" said Salvador.

Orlando

by Nat Gabriel
illustrated by Mike Reed

Scott Foresman

Editorial Offices: Glenview, Illinois • New York, New York
Sales Offices: Reading, Massachusetts • Duluth, Georgia
Glenview, Illinois • Carrollton, Texas • Menlo Park, California

Salvador was upset. He told
Mama he was going out. He didn't
want her to be worried or sad. He
just needed to be alone.

Orlando led Salvador home. They
ran through the cornfield as fast as
they could go. Mama stood by the
door on the porch.

"Oh, Salvador. I was so worried!"
she cried.

Before long Salvador heard a
snorting sound. It was Orlando!
Orlando had come to find him!
Salvador reached out for Orlando.
He felt the pig's ear. He held on.

He hurried across the cornfield.
He turned the corner of the fort and
ran through the door. No one
would see or hear him cry.

The floor was just dirt, but
Salvador liked his fort. He had
made it himself the year before. He
had brought wood scraps from the
old barn behind his house.

Salvador got up and ran out of
the fort. It was dark! He couldn't see.
He did not know which way
was home.

Next Salvador heard a loud
crack! Lightning had struck a tree in
the forest. The tree was on fire!

Salvador lay down on the dirt floor. He closed his eyes. He had a picture in his mind of his mama. He thought about what had happened at home before he left. He cried some more.

As Salvador lay in the fort crying, it began to rain. At first it was only a light rain. Then it began to pour. Next there was lightning and thunder. It was a very bad storm!

Salvador adored Orlando.
Orlando was four years old.
Salvador had named him after a
place in Florida he had read about.
There could not be a more perfect
pet for Salvador.

"We have to sell Orlando," Mama
had said.
Salvador had put down his fork.
"What did you say, Mama?"
Mama tried to explain. But she
could not bring herself to say more.
She just looked away.

"Why would we sell Orlando?" Salvador had asked.

"You know we are moving, Salvador. And we will not have room for him at our new place. I know he is a fine pig," Mama had said.

"Orlando is more than a pig!" Salvador had shouted. "He is family."

"I know, son," Mama had said. "If anyone tries to take poor Orlando, I won't let them!" Salvador had shouted. Then he had hurried from the house to his fort.

Grade 2
Phonics Reader 15

What Could It Be?
by Judy Nayer
illustrated by
Bob Berry

Phonics Skills:
• Vowel patterns
  oo, ou
• Comparative endings
  -er, -est

Scott Foresman
Phonics System

Scott Foresman

What Could It Be?

by Judy Nayer
illustrated by Bob Berry

This book belongs to

_____

Phonics for Families: This book features words with the vowel sound heard in *good* and *could*, and words with the comparative endings *-er* and *-est*. It also provides practice reading the high-frequency words *beautiful*, *become*, *even*, *great*, and *together*. Have your child read the book to you. Then say a word such as *big*, and have your child say the comparative words that can be made from the word (*bigger*, *biggest*).

Phonics Skills: Vowel patterns *oo*, *ou*; Comparative endings *-er*, *-est*

High-Frequency Words: *beautiful*, *become*, *even*, *great*, *together*

"Meet my beautiful new puppy!"

What Could It Be?

by Judy Nayer
illustrated by Bob Berry

Scott Foresman

Editorial Offices: Glenview, Illinois • New York, New York
Sales Offices: Reading, Massachusetts • Duluth, Georgia
Glenview, Illinois • Carrollton, Texas • Menlo Park, California

Ann took longer than she
should have.
Grace stood and tapped her foot.

the most beautiful, cuddliest, softest, and furriest, greatest new friend for you and me!"

When Ann came out, she had a box.
Grace tried to take a look.

"What is it? What is it?
What could it be?
Would you open it up?
Let me look and see!"

"I know what you are thinking.
But it just could not be.
So come a little closer
and you will see . . .

4

13

"It's something that can grow?
Oh, that is good to know!
If it can grow, it could become
the largest thing I know!"

"Oh, no! Don't look!
You must try to guess.
You should ask me some things.
I'll say no or yes."

"Is it bigger than a fly?
Is it smaller than a book?
Is it something made of wood?
Is it something great to cook?"

"It could be, but it isn't.
It is not something to throw.
It's now no longer than a foot.
But it's something that will grow!"

6

11

© Scott Foresman 2

"It's not the biggest
or the smallest thing.
That much I should know.
We could play with it together.
Is it a great big ball to throw?"

"It's bigger than a fly.
It's even larger than a book.
It's much softer than wood.
It would not be good to cook!"

"If I shook it, would it break?
Is it beautiful to see?
Can we play with it together?
Would you please show me?"

"The answers you are looking
for are no, yes, and yes!
Should I show you?
No, I shouldn't.
I still want you to guess!"

Grade 2
Phonics Reader 16

Timmy's Ears
by Gloria Dominic
illustrated by
Gary Colby

Phonics Skills:
- *R*-controlled vowels
  ear, eer
- Suffix *-ly*

Scott Foresman

Timmy's Ears

by Gloria Dominic
illustrated by Gary Colby

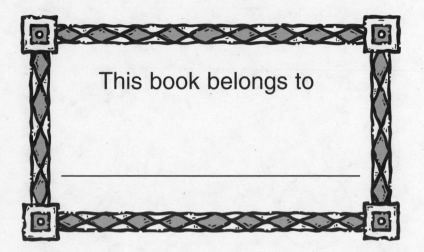

This book belongs to

_____

Phonics for Families: This book gives your child practice reading words that contain the vowel sound heard in *ear* and *cheer* and words that end with the suffix *-ly*. It also features the high-frequency words *ago, better, head, idea,* and *still*. After reading the book together, ask your child to name some words that rhyme with *ear*.

Phonics Skills: *R*-controlled vowels *ear, eer*; Suffix *-ly*

High-Frequency Words: *ago, better, head, idea, still*

Timmy's head came up first. He happily cheered, "I can hear clearly! There is no more water in my ears!"

"What?" asked Mary. "I can't hear you. There's water in my ears!"

16

Timmy's Ears

by Gloria Dominic
illustrated by Gary Colby

Scott Foresman

Editorial Offices: Glenview, Illinois • New York, New York
Sales Offices: Reading, Massachusetts • Duluth, Georgia
Glenview, Illinois • Carrollton, Texas • Menlo Park, California

One hot summer day, not long
ago, Timmy called his friend Mary.
"It is a lovely day," said Timmy.
"The sun is shining brightly. The sky
is clear and blue."

"Dear, dear!" said Judy. "I know
how to get the water out of your ears.
Watch this."
Judy did a silly trick. And one by
one, they fell into the water.

"This happened to me a long time ago," said Nicky. "I have a better idea." But sadly, it didn't work either.

"It is a lovely day," said Mary. "Let's go swimming at the lake near your house!"
"Good idea!" said Timmy.

The two friends got ready quickly. Mary packed a ball, an umbrella, and some towels. Timmy got a blanket and some sandwiches.

Soon, Timmy and Mary were happily walking to the lake with their gear.

By this time, Timmy and Mary's friends were trying to help. Each one had an idea about how to get the water out of Timmy's ears.

"Have no fear! I can help you,"
said Mary. "Do this! The water will
come out quickly."

She began jumping on one foot.
She slowly shook her head to the side
as she jumped.

Timmy started jumping too. He
shook his head slowly as he jumped.
But the water still did not come out.

"Last one in is a rotten egg!" Timmy
yelled loudly.

He jumped into the water with
a giant splash.

Mary cheered!

"Watch this," said Mary as she
jumped in.

All morning long, the two friends happily played in the clear, chilly water. They twisted and flipped all around. They kept jumping off the dock to see who could make the biggest splash. And they threw the ball quickly back and forth in the water.

Mary shook her head slowly and laughed. "Oh, dear," she said, moving closer to Timmy. "I know why you can't hear me. You have water in your ears!"

"It's still not very clear," said Timmy.

"You have water in your ears!" yelled Mary.

"I can't hear you," said Timmy.

"Do you want lunch?" Mary asked.
"You want a bunch?" said Timmy.
"A bunch of what?"
"No!" said Mary. "I want lunch now!"
"You want a bunch of cows?"
asked Timmy, looking puzzled.

Mary and Timmy had so much fun!
They laughed so hard that tears rolled
down their cheeks.

Suddenly, Mary's stomach was growling hungrily.

When Timmy's head came up out of the water, Mary called to him.

"Timmy," she said, "do you want to eat lunch now?"

Timmy grinned, but did not answer her.

"Timmy," Mary said again, "do you want to eat now?"

Timmy still did not answer.

Mary was getting upset. In a louder voice, she asked, "Timmy, can you hear me?"

"What?" said Timmy. "I can't hear you."

Scott Foresman
Reading

Grade 2
Phonics Reader 17

**Joyce, Who
Hated Noise**
by Claire Daniel
illustrated by
Chuck Gonzales

Phonics Skills:
• Vowel diphthongs *oi, oy*
• Suffix *-ful*

Scott Foresman
**Phonics
System**

Scott Foresman

Joyce, Who Hated Noise

by Claire Daniel
illustrated by Chuck Gonzales

This book belongs to

_____

Phonics for Families: This book gives your child practice in reading words that contain the vowel sound heard in *noise* and *boys* and words with the suffix *-ful*. It also features the high-frequency words *about*, *father*, *different*, and *important*. After you and your child read the book together, make a list of words that contain the vowel diphthongs *oi* and *oy*.

Phonics Skills: vowel diphthongs *oi*, *oy*; Suffix *-ful*

High-Frequency Words: *about*, *father*, *different*, *important*

To this day, Joyce lives in a very noisy kingdom. And she likes it that way!

16

Joyce, Who Hated Noise

by Claire Daniel
illustrated by Chuck Gonzales

Scott Foresman

Editorial Offices: Glenview, Illinois • New York, New York
Sales Offices: Reading, Massachusetts • Duluth, Georgia
Glenview, Illinois • Carrollton, Texas • Menlo Park, California

Not long ago, there was a princess named Joyce who hated noise. Every morning it was so noisy, she had no choice but to wake up.

"There is too much noise!" Princess Joyce cried.

Joyce laughed. She enjoyed the different noises her voice made.

Troy and Roy asked her to join them in a race. Joyce said yes. She knew they would let her make a lot of noise.

Honk

Plink

"Father," Joyce said, "I think a little noise would be okay. I don't like it when there is no noise."

"Joyce," her father said.

Joyce cried, "I can't hear you!"

Then Joyce shook her head. Corn fell out of her ears. Floyd barked as the corn hit the floor.

"What a wonderful sound!" Joyce said.

The rooster crowed. Two noisy boys, Roy and Troy, ran into her room on their way to play.

"Noise even spoils the sunrise!" Joyce cried.

She got up and went to see her father the king about it.

"Father!" she said. "This kingdom is too noisy. Wouldn't it be wonderful without noise?"

"It would be peaceful," her father said. "But I can't do anything about noise. A little noise is not harmful."

"But, Father, this is important!" she said. "Very important!"

"Not now, Joyce," he said. "I have to work. And you need to take Floyd the royal dog out for a walk. Now be careful."

Days passed. Every day was the same. Nothing was different. The rooster crowed. Joyce could not hear it. Roy and Troy ran and played. Joyce did not hear them.

Princess Joyce was unhappy. She couldn't even enjoy the sunrise that filled her room each morning.

Princess Joyce rushed in to see her father. She wanted to share the good news with him. There was no more noise in the kingdom!

Her father did not understand. He heard noise. He tried to talk to her. But she couldn't hear him.

Joyce took Floyd out for a walk. On her way out, she walked by a man counting stacks of gold coins.

"Plop, plop, clink, clink!" The coins made so much noise.

"You're too noisy!" Joyce told the man. But the man did not stop counting.

She walked by Roy and Troy who were playing with their toys.

"You're too noisy, boys!" she told them. But Roy and Troy did not stop playing.

Princess Joyce could not hear the men lifting the piano. She could not hear the man counting his coins. She could not hear Roy and Troy and their toys.

Princess Joyce could not hear a thing! She was joyful!

Princess Joyce had corn in her crown. She had corn on her dress. She had corn in her mouth. She had corn in her ears.

"Are you all right?" everyone asked.

Princess Joyce did not hear the people. She stood up. She stepped away from the corn. Then she picked up Floyd's leash and headed home.

Joyce walked by two men who were lifting a huge piano.

"Heave, ho!" they shouted.

"You're making too much noise!" Joyce cried.

But the men kept working. They shouted over her voice.

Then Floyd saw a cat. Floyd broke free and chased the cat. The cat ran toward the chickens. They began to make a lot of noise.

The chickens flew on top of a mule. The noisy chickens scared the mule. The mule kicked over a cart full of corn. A sack of corn landed on top of the princess.

Scott Foresman Reading

Grade 2
Phonics Reader 18

**The Gingerbread
Bakers**
by Amy Moses
illustrated by
Vicki Woodworth

Phonics Skills:
- Short *e* spelled *ea*
- Suffix *-er*

Scott Foresman
Phonics System

Scott Foresman

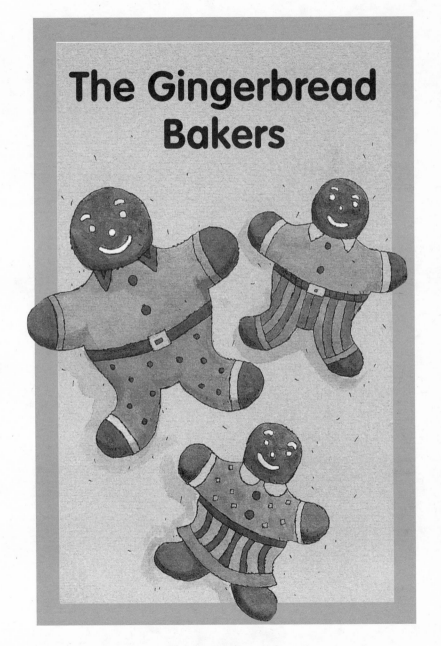

The Gingerbread Bakers

by Amy Moses
illustrated by Vicki Woodworth

This book belongs to

_____

Phonics for Families: This book features words with short *e* spelled *ea*, as in *ready* and *gingerbread*; words that end with the letters *er*, as in *mixer* and *baker;* and the high-frequency words *large, ready, today,* and *wash.* Read the book together. Then encourage your child to talk about a time he or she helped someone.

Phonics Skill: Short *e* spelled *ea*; Suffix *-er*
High-Frequency Words: *large, ready, today, wash*

Grandpa laughed. "Who is ready to be a gingerbread eater?"

"We are! We are!" they all cried.

Grandpa picked up a plate of gingerbread. He always made some for his helpers. "Now the gingerbread bakers are gingerbread eaters!" he said.

The Gingerbread Bakers

by Amy Moses
illustrated by Vicki Woodworth

Scott Foresman

Editorial Offices: Glenview, Illinois • New York, New York
Sales Offices: Reading, Massachusetts • Duluth, Georgia
Glenview, Illinois • Carrollton, Texas • Menlo Park, California

The clock rang. Ned ran into
Heather's room. "Get ready!" he yelled.

"Come back later," Heather groaned.

"But Heather," said Ned, "it's time
to get ready. We're Grandpa's
helpers today."

2

"What would you like to eat today?"
Grandpa asked.

"Gingerbread!" they all shouted.

"How about cornbread instead?"
asked Grandpa.

"No!" they all cried.

"How about shortbread?" he asked.

"No!" they all said. "We want to eat
gingerbread!"

15

Heather and Ned were happy. They were gingerbread bakers!

"I know," said Heather. "But I'm a sleepyhead." She stretched. Then she kicked off her bedspread and climbed out of bed.

Heather looked out the window.

It was dark. She got dressed and ran downstairs.

Ned, Mom, and Dad were ready to go.
They were waiting for Heather. Dad was
holding a bag of cookie cutters.

4

Heather and Ned drew feathers on
the birds. They drew berries on the
trees. They drew faces on the people.

13

After a while, Heather and Ned called, "It's ready. The gingerbread is ready."

While the gingerbread cooled, Ned and Heather made icing.

They all piled into the car. They were going to help Grandpa make gingerbread. Grandpa is a baker.

When they got to the shop, Grandpa gave everyone a big kiss on the forehead. "What would you like to bake today?" Grandpa asked.

"Gingerbread!" they all shouted.

© Scott Foresman 2

"I'm going to be a gingerbread watcher," Heather said.

"I'm going to be a gingerbread watcher too," cried Ned. "We will tell you when it's ready."

Grandpa set the timer on the large oven.

They used rolling pins to make the dough flat. Then everyone chose a cookie cutter and started to cut out shapes. When everyone was finished, Grandpa put the gingerbread shapes on baking trays.

"How about cornbread instead?" asked Grandpa.

"No!" they all cried.

"How about shortbread?" he asked.

"No!" they all said. "We want to make gingerbread!"

Grandpa laughed. "Go wash your hands."

Grandpa read the cookbook.
Heather put the flour into a large bowl.
Ned added the spices. Mom put in the
honey. Dad added the eggs. Then
Grandpa turned on the mixer.

When the dough was ready,
Grandpa scraped it out of the bowl.
He cut it into smaller pieces.

Scott Foresman
Reading

Grade 2
Phonics Reader 19

**The Best Baseball
Players**
by Robin Bloksberg
illustrated by
Robert Lawson

Phonics Skills:
- /ȯ/ Vowel patterns
  al, au
- Silent letter patterns
  gh, kn, mb

Scott Foresman
**Phonics
System**

Scott Foresman

The Best
Baseball Players

by Robin Bloksberg
illustrated by Robert Lawson

This book belongs to

_____

Phonics for Families: This book provides practice reading words with the vowel patterns *al* and *au*, as in *ball* and *because;* words with the silent letter patterns *gh, kn,* and *mb,* as in *high, know,* and *climb;* and the high-frequency words *able, early, own, story,* and *thought.* After reading the book together, have your child go back through the story and point out and read the words with the vowel patterns *al* and *au* and the words with the silent letter patterns *gh, kn,* and *mb.*

Phonics Skills: /ȯ/ Vowel patterns *al, au;* Silent letter patterns *gh, kn, mb*

High-Frequency Words: *able, early, own, story, thought*

Maybe someday you'll be able to hit a baseball very high and very straight. Or maybe you'll be a very good catcher.

And then maybe your own name will be in the Baseball Hall of Fame!

16

The Best Baseball Players

by Robin Bloksberg
illustrated by Robert Lawson

Scott Foresman

Editorial Offices: Glenview, Illinois • New York, New York
Sales Offices: Reading, Massachusetts • Duluth, Georgia
Glenview, Illinois • Carrollton, Texas • Menlo Park, California

Since baseball was first played more than two hundred years ago, there have been many good baseball players. There have also been some great ballplayers.

The best ballplayers of all are part of the Baseball Hall of Fame.

The baseball players in the Hall of Fame worked hard to be the best. But there is something else they all did too.

They all loved playing baseball.

At the Hall of Fame, you can walk around. You can see many things from the early days of baseball.

You can see old baseball bats. You can see old baseball caps and baseball gloves. You can even climb the steps and see some old ballpark seats.

Babe Ruth

This baseball player knew how to hit a ball. He could knock balls high up in the air. He would hit them right out of the ballpark.

He hit 714 home runs in his lifetime. That's why he is in the Hall of Fame.

Ty Cobb

It's not good to steal, unless you're in a baseball game. Then it might be all right to steal bases.

This baseball player was able to steal more bases than just about anyone. In one year, he stole ninety-six bases. That put him into the Hall of Fame.

© Scott Foresman 2

The Baseball Hall of Fame is in New York State.

Some day you might go there. You can learn all about the story of baseball.

Willie Mays

When this baseball player was little, his father taught him how to throw a ball. When he grew up, he was able to catch well too.

He was the first baseball player to hit three hundred home runs and steal three hundred bases. Now he is in the Baseball Hall of Fame.

Mickey Mantle

This baseball player knew how to hit balls straight over the ballpark walls. He could bat with his right or his left hand. People thought that was great! He, too, is in the Baseball Hall of Fame.

Yogi Berra

A long time ago, this baseball player caught balls better than anyone else did. People still talk about him. Because of this, his story is told in the Hall of Fame.

Most great baseball players make the game look very easy. But it takes hard work and skill to be a good baseball player. It helps to start playing early.

Lou Gehrig

The story of this baseball player is just as great! He played 2,130 baseball games in a row. He didn't miss one!

Because of this, he landed in the Baseball Hall of Fame.

Great ballplayers don't play alone. They know that to be a great baseball player, you have to be able to get along with others. You have to be part of a team.

Jackie Robinson

This baseball player liked to play football, basketball, tennis, and golf. But he is best known as a baseball player.

He was the first African American to play ball in the major leagues. Now he is in the Hall of Fame.

8

Roberto Clemente

When people saw this baseball player walk onto a ballfield, they always cheered. As a professional baseball player, he had three thousand hits. His fans thought he was the greatest. Now he is in the Hall of Fame too.

9

Scott Foresman
Reading

Grade 2
Phonics Reader 20

Fawn at Dawn
by Maggie Bridger
illustrated by
Lane Yerkes

Phonics Skills:
• /ȯ/ vowel patterns
  aw, ough
• Silent letter patterns
  gn, wh, wr

Scott Foresman
**Phonics
System**

Scott Foresman

by Maggie Bridger
illustrated by Lane Yerkes

This book belongs to

_____

Phonics for Families: This book features words with the vowel patterns *aw*, as in *fawn*, and *ough* as in *thought*; and words with silent letters, as in *sign*, *wrote*, and *whole*. It also gives your child practice reading the high-frequency words *family*, *finally*, *morning*, *paper*, and *really*. After reading this book together, talk about something surprising your family has seen.

Phonics Skills: /ȯ/ Vowel patterns *aw*, *ough*; Silent letter patterns *gn*, *wh*, *wr*

High-Frequency Words: *really*, *morning*, *paper*, *finally*, *family*

And I wasn't alone either. My whole family was with me. Finally, we all saw the fawn. We really did!

16

Fawn at Dawn

by Maggie Bridger
illustrated by Lane Yerkes

Scott Foresman

Editorial Offices: Glenview, Illinois • New York, New York
Sales Offices: Reading, Massachusetts • Duluth, Georgia
Glenview, Illinois • Carrollton, Texas • Menlo Park, California

I saw a fawn yesterday. I really, really did!

I woke up early and looked out my window. There on the lawn was a tiny spotted fawn.

I didn't move. I didn't even yawn. But, suddenly, it was gone.

The fawn was there. It wasn't a shadow. It wasn't leaves by the seesaw. And it wasn't alone. Its mother was eating the lawn too.

The next morning I woke up at
dawn. I wrapped a shawl around me.
I tiptoed to the window. I looked out.

I told my brother. He didn't
believe me.

"You thought you saw a fawn,"
he said.

"I saw a fawn. I really, really
did!" I said.

"It was probably just a shadow,"
Paul said.

I told my mother.

"Oh, dear," Mom said. "I ought to have the doctor look at your eyes. Maybe you need glasses."

"I saw a fawn! I really, really did!" I said.

"It was probably just some leaves by the seesaw," Mom said.

It had been an awful day. I wrote in my book, "I thought I saw a fawn. I hope I did. But now I don't know for sure."

Then I went to bed.

But we had no straw. And Mom hadn't bought any berries this week.

"Fawns like salt," Paul said.

I put some salt on the lawn, but it felt all wrong.

I told my father.

At first, I didn't think he even heard me. He was reading the morning paper.

"I saw a fawn. I really, really did!" I said.

This was awful. No one in my family believed me!

Then Dad put his paper down.

"Well, Jenny, can you draw a picture of what you saw?"

Maybe I could design a perfect spot for a fawn. I could make a straw bed. I could find food it likes. I know fawns like berries. Then maybe the fawn would smell the berries and come back.

I sat back. My knees hurt. My wrists hurt. I was a wreck!

Who would ever believe me now? I gnawed at my fingernails. Then I got another idea!

I tried, but it came out all wrong. I tried again. I filled nine whole pages. But I couldn't make my picture look like the fawn I had seen.

Finally, I got an idea!

Maybe if I went out on the lawn and crawled around, I might find a sign that the fawn had been there.

I crawled around the seesaw.

I crawled near the garden.

I found nothing!

"What are you doing?" Paul asked me.

"I'm looking for paw prints from the fawn," I said.

My brother shook his head. "Are you sure you saw a fawn?" he asked. "Fawns don't have paws. You ought to know that!"

Scott Foresman
Reading

Grade 2
Phonics Reader 21

**Touchdown at
Space Camp**
by Judy Veramendi
illustrated by
Tom Barrett

Phonics Skills:
• Short *u* spelled *ou*
• Multisyllabic words

Scott Foresman
Phonics System

Scott Foresman

by Judy Veramendi
illustrated by Tom Barrett

This book belongs to

_____

Phonics for Families: This book gives practice reading words with short *u* spelled *ou*, as in *touch*; words with more than two syllables; and the high-frequency words *began*, *Earth*, *ever*, *remember*, and *try*. Read the book together. Then have your child read aloud the story words with short *u* spelled *ou*.

Phonics Skill: Short *u* spelled *ou*; Multisyllabic words

High-Frequency Words: *began*, *Earth*, *ever*, *remember*, *try*

Space Camp

Space Camp teaches kids about space. But it also teaches kids to work together and always try their best!

16

Touchdown at Space Camp

by Judy Veramendi
illustrated by Tom Barrett

Scott Foresman

Editorial Offices: Glenview, Illinois • New York, New York
Sales Offices: Reading, Massachusetts • Duluth, Georgia
Glenview, Illinois • Carrollton, Texas • Menlo Park, California

Did you ever think about being an astronaut some day?

You don't have to wait for years and years. You can try a trip on the space shuttle right now, at Space Camp!

After a week of working together, the campers get ready to go home. Many campers stay in touch with the friends they make at Space Camp.

The campers are happy doing the jobs they are asked to do. They know that each job is very important.

The first Space Camp began in 1982. The man who started this camp got his idea from a rocket scientist.

This scientist felt that children might like a camp where they are trained just like astronauts.

The scientist was right! More than 25,000 children have gone to Space Camp since the opening of the first camp in 1982.

Camps in Florida and in other countries followed that first Space Camp. Children of all ages from all over the world have enjoyed their stay at Space Camp.

Six campers form the land crew and watch over the flight. Another six campers form the flight crew. They will take the trip into space!

Finally it's the time the campers have been waiting for. They will take a trip on the shuttle!

They have worked hard all week. They are ready!

Children spend one week at Space Camp. It is a week filled with learning and fun!

In one week all the campers get to know what it's really like to be an astronaut—without ever leaving Earth!

When the campers first get to
camp, they meet other young
kids from all over the country. At
check-in, the campers find out where
and with whom they will live for the
next week. Then the roommates
double up to form bunkmates. The
rooms are called bays and have
names like Earth and Mars.

Have you ever thought about living
on the moon? These campers have!

They spend a day setting up their
own moon base. Each camper is
dressed in a spacesuit. The campers
learn that they must work together
to get their jobs done.

After spending a tough day on
the "moon," they are happy to go
back to their bays!

Campers try moving underwater.
Did you ever try walking in a
pool or lake? Do you remember
how it felt?

Moving underwater is very much
like floating in space.

One of the first places the campers
visit is Rocket Park. Here they get to
see real rockets.

After seeing the real rockets, the campers try making their own little rockets. They will use crickets as astronauts. They work long and hard to make good rockets for their bugs. The campers don't want their "astronauts" to have a rough flight!

8

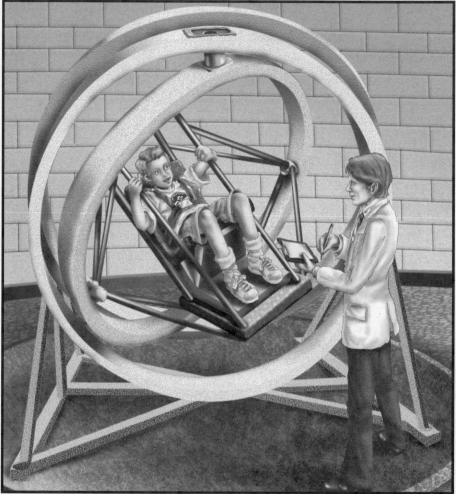

On another day, the campers get in a chair that tosses them five different ways. This chair gives them an idea of what it is like to be floating in space.

9

Scott Foresman
Reading

Grade 2
Phonics Reader 22

Paul and His Blue Ox
retold by Jan M. Mike
illustrated by
Catherine Kanner

Phonics Skills:
• Schwa sound
• Plurals -s and -es

Scott Foresman
Phonics
System

Scott Foresman

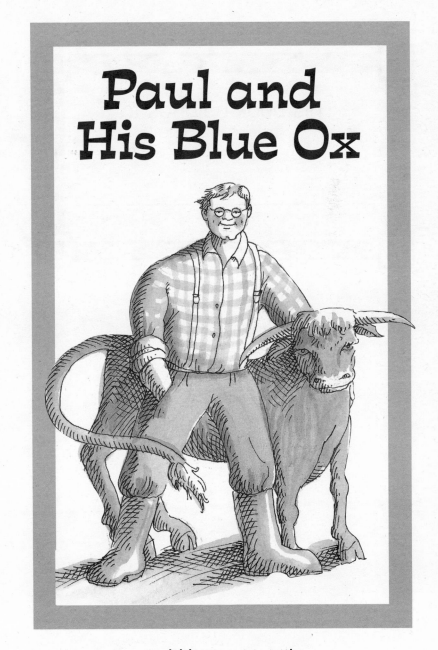

Paul and His Blue Ox

retold by Jan M. Mike
illustrated by Catherine Kanner

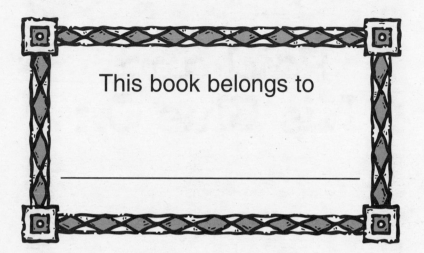

This book belongs to

_____

Phonics for Families: This book features words that have the vowel sound heard in the beginning of *across* and at the end of *people*; words in which the letter *s* was added to form a plural and in doing so created a new syllable, as in the word *houses*; and words in which the letters *es* were added to form a plural, as in *boxes*, *peaches*, *eyelashes*, and *glasses*. It also provides practice reading the high-frequency words *behind, only, sure, upon,* and *word*. Read the book together. Then talk about all the exaggerated details in this story.

Phonics Skills: Schwa sound; Plurals *-s* and *-es*

High-Frequency Words: *behind, only, sure, upon, word*

Paul Bunyan didn't mind a bit.
Babe was just his size. And best of all,
Paul wasn't alone any more. For the
first time, Paul Bunyan had a friend!

16

Paul and His Blue Ox

retold by Jan M. Mike
illustrated by Catherine Kanner

Scott Foresman

Editorial Offices: Glenview, Illinois • New York, New York
Sales Offices: Reading, Massachusetts • Duluth, Georgia
Glenview, Illinois • Carrollton, Texas • Menlo Park, California

Long ago, Paul Bunyan lived right around here. Paul Bunyan was a big man. He was a very big man.

Babe grew. She grew until she almost filled the whole cabin. She was now a very big ox.

2

15

Paul Bunyan carried the ox home
to his simple cabin. He named her
Babe. He fed her wagons of warm
milk, hills of hay, and boxes of
peaches.

Paul Bunyan was so big, he stood
taller than the tallest trees. A big
church steeple just tickled his belly.

Paul was huge! His glasses were bigger than tire wheels. His eyelashes were so long he had to curl them. He brushed tangles out of his hair with a tree. And he used a big tree as a toothpick!

Paul lifted the ox out of the snow. The ox was so cold she was blue. Paul let her snuggle inside his jacket.

Paul Bunyan heard the noises again. He was sure they were coming from under the snow. He dug down. It was a baby ox. She was as cold as an icicle. And she was big.

People sit on benches. But Paul Bunyan sat upon the tallest hill. A small hill behind his bed was his pillow. A large river rippled by near Paul's home. But it was only a foot bath for him.

Paul had to be careful. After all, just one sneeze could blow away three houses!

One day his nose began to itch. He scratched and scratched. When he was done, he had knocked down one hundred trees.

The noises came from across the lake. Paul didn't waste time. He went ahead. He crossed the frozen water.

Paul Bunyan went walking in the
blue snow. Then he heard some very
strange noises. The noises sounded
like a baby crying, only much
deeper.

Paul used the trees to make a
simple cabin. He liked the cabin.
Now Paul had just about everything
he could want. There was only one
thing he didn't have. He didn't have
a friend.

Winter came. It was a terrible winter. A horrible winter! It was so cold the cooking fires froze solid.

It was so cold that people skated on frozen air. If you said a word, it was sure to freeze as you said it.

It was so cold that the snow all around turned blue. That is why they called it the winter of the blue snow.

Scott Foresman Reading

Grade 2
Phonics Reader 23

The Statue of Liberty
by Anastasia Suen

Phonics Skills:
• Vowel digraph *ue*
• Schwa sound in *weather*

Scott Foresman Phonics System

Scott Foresman

The Statue of Liberty

by Anastasia Suen

This book belongs to

_____

Phonics for Families: This book provides practice reading words with the vowel sound heard at the end of *statue* and *true* and words that contain the sound heard at the end of *plaster*. It also features the high-frequency words *course, hear, things,* and *years*. Read the book together. Then work with your child to list other words that contain the *ue* sound.

Phonics Skills: Vowel digraph *ue*; Schwa sound in *weather*

High-Frequency Words: *course, hear, things, years*

The Statue of Liberty was a true
gift. It reminds us all of our freedom.

16

The Statue of Liberty

by Anastasia Suen

Scott Foresman

Editorial Offices: Glenview, Illinois • New York, New York
Sales Offices: Reading, Massachusetts • Duluth, Georgia
Glenview, Illinois • Carrollton, Texas • Menlo Park, California

Do you know which statue was a birthday present? Here's a clue. It has to do with liberty.

Yes. It's the Statue of Liberty. France gave it to the U.S.A. years and years ago.

© Scott Foresman 2

Then the Statue of Liberty was put together. It took six months to build. On October 28, 1886, the Statue of Liberty stood in New York Harbor.

The artist wanted the statue to be high above the ground. But the base of the statue was not ready. Many people gave money to build the base.

Frédéric-Auguste Bartholdi

This French artist liked large statues. He wanted to build a statue that would celebrate liberty. *Liberty* is another word for freedom.

The artist wanted his statue to stand in New York Harbor, looking over the blue water.

4

In 1885, a ship carrying the Statue of Liberty sailed into New York Harbor. It carried over two hundred crates of numbered pieces.

13

In 1884, the Statue of Liberty was finished. The French people wanted to give America the statue on its birthday, July 4. But the statue had to be taken apart to be shipped. So the birthday gift would not arrive on time.

Deciding how the statue would look took time. The artist worked on small clay models. Of course, he tried many things.

Finally, the artist drew the statue. Some people say the statue's face looks like his mother. Others argue that it does not.

On an avenue in Paris, the statue grew taller. The artist was happy to hear that the statue would stand in New York Harbor.

Two years later, Liberty's head was on display in Paris. The head was hollow. People climbed inside. They looked out of the crown, just as they do today.

Of course, the artist did not make the statue himself. Many workers made plaster models. The workers made larger and larger models. Finally they were the size he wanted.

Next they put thin sheets of copper over the plaster. Later these sheets were bolted together to form the statue.

8

In 1876, the torch from the Statue of Liberty arrived in America. The rest of the statue was not ready yet. It was America's one-hundredth birthday. Red, white, and blue flags flew everywhere.

9

Scott Foresman
Reading

Grade 2
Phonics Reader 24

**Great Sunday
Sleigh Rides**
by Sydnie Meltzer Kleinhenz
illustrated by
Lauren Klementz-Harte

Phonics Skills:
• Long *a* spelled *ei*
• Multisyllabic words
(words with endings
and suffixes)

Scott Foresman
**Phonics
System**

Scott Foresman

Great Sunday
Sleigh Rides

by Sydnie Meltzer Kleinhenz
illustrated by Lauren Klementz-Harte

This book belongs to

_____

Phonics for Families: In this book, your child will practice reading words with long *a* spelled *ei*, as in *sleigh*; words with more than one syllable that have endings and suffixes, as in *invited* and *suddenly*; and the high-frequency words *move, near, cold,* and *grow*. Read the story together. Then talk about how Leila had to fit the pieces of the puzzle together to find a solution.

Phonics Skills: Long *a* spelled *ei*; Multisyllabic words (words with endings and suffixes)

High-Frequency Words: *move, near, cold, grow*

Great Sunday Sleigh Rides

by Sydnie Meltzer Kleinhenz

illustrated by Lauren Klementz-Harte

Scott Foresman

Editorial Offices: Glenview, Illinois • New York, New York
Sales Offices: Reading, Massachusetts • Duluth, Georgia
Glenview, Illinois • Carrollton, Texas • Menlo Park, California

"Thanks for another great sleigh ride," the mayor said. Friends and neighbors shouted thanks to Norm. Then they headed to the house for a hot drink. Everyone was cold!

© Scott Foresman 2

The next day, Mac and the sleigh came to Grandpop's. The Perkinses brought a load of feed.

"We asked the mayor to help," Ross said. "He invited everyone to his house after the sleigh rides." Leila danced around thanking everyone.

Then she took the reins and led Mac to his new home.

Leila sighed. Grandpop had a home
for Mac, but no feed. The Perkinses had
feed, but no home. Suddenly, it all
fit together!

Leila helped her little brother give
Mac a carrot. "Keep your hand open,"
Leila said.

Mac neighed. Sam giggled at the
bells on the reins.

Leila and Sam joined the other people in Norm's house. Everyone was talking happily. They were talking about how much they liked the sleigh rides. Leila said, "I can't wait until my next ride!"

When Leila got home, she sat on the porch. She didn't mind the cold evening air. She just thought about Mac. She thought about how much she wanted to keep him. It all seemed hopeless now.

"I would love to keep Mac in town," said Peg. "Ross and I could give him free feed. But we don't have a place for a horse and sleigh. We store things in the shed."

Leila was upset. She could hardly see through her tears.

Norm joined his neighbors and friends. People cheered. He smiled sadly and put up his hands.

"Neighbors," he said, "tonight ends forty-eight years of sleigh rides. I am moving. I am going to move near my daughter."

Leila ran outside with tears running
down her cheeks. She put her arms around
Mac. He nuzzled her.

"I'll miss you," Leila said.

"How can I help?" asked Peg.

"I need a place to keep him and a
way to feed him. Could he and the
sleigh stay out back?" Leila asked. "I
would care for him every morning,
and work every afternoon to pay for
his feed."

Leila walked slowly into the Perkinses' feed store. She saw Peg weighing a bag. Ross was stacking boxes.

Peg looked up. "Hi, Leila. You look really sad. Can I help you?" she asked.

Leila cleared her throat. "Will you please help me keep Mac in town?" She crossed her fingers hopefully.

Early Monday morning, Leila went to see Mac. He neighed and she patted his side. "I wish you were mine," Leila said.

Just then Norm came in. He put his hand on Leila's head. "I know you love Mac. I would like you to have him, if you can think of a way to keep him," he said.

That night, Leila asked Dad about keeping Mac. "Can we keep him in the backyard? I would care for him and you could give the sleigh rides."

"I would love to give sleigh rides," Dad said. "But the sleigh needs a shed and Mac needs a bigger space."

Leila frowned. "I have to think of a way to keep him," she said.

The next afternoon, Leila went to Grandpop's farm. "Grandpop," she said. "Can you help me? Norm said I can keep Mac, but our yard is too little. Can he stay on your farm? Can you keep him and his sleigh in your barn?"

Grandpop rubbed his chin and said, "I would love to give Mac a home, but I can't pay for all his feed."

© Scott Foresman 2

Scott Foresman
Reading

Grade 2
Phonics Reader 25

Extinct!
by F. R. Robinson
illustrated by
Allan Cormack

Phonics Skills:
- Pattern *ex*
- Prefixes *un-*, *dis-*, *re-*

Scott Foresman
Phonics System

Scott Foresman

by F. R. Robinson
illustrated by Allan Cormack

This book belongs to

Phonics for Families: This book gives your child practice reading words with the letters *ex*, as in *expert* and *next*; words with the prefixes *dis-*, *un-*, and *re-*, as in *display*, *unlike*, and *remove*; and the high-frequency words *along*, *front*, and *right*. Read the book together. Then have your child read aloud the words with *ex*.

Phonics Skills: Pattern *ex*; Prefixes *un-*, *dis-*, *re-*

High-Frequency Words: *along*, *front*, *right*

But they do agree that it was a good thing someone discovered that first tooth! We have learned many things about these exciting animals! Who knows what we'll find out next!

Extinct!

by F. R. Robinson
illustrated by Allan Cormack

Scott Foresman

Editorial Offices: Glenview, Illinois • New York, New York
Sales Offices: Reading, Massachusetts • Duluth, Georgia
Glenview, Illinois • Carrollton, Texas • Menlo Park, California

Dinosaurs lived long ago. There are no dinosaurs now. They are extinct. That means they are no longer around.

Then how do we know they ever existed? People have found their bones!

Why did the dinosaurs disappear? Dinosaur bones can't explain that. Experts disagree about what caused the dinosaurs to die.

We know that dinosaurs hatched
from eggs. Sometimes a baby
dinosaur is found along with its egg.

In 1822, Mary Ann Mantell found
a huge tooth. She showed it to Mr.
Mantell. He saved things like that.

Mr. Mantell looked at the tooth.
He said that it probably came from
a huge animal. This animal was
unlike any kind of animal alive
then, or now.

4

Some dinosaurs ate meat.
Others ate plants. Experts can tell
what dinosaurs ate by looking at
their teeth.

13

Some dinosaurs were huge. Others were small. Some walked on four legs. Some walked on two legs, with their front legs up off the ground.

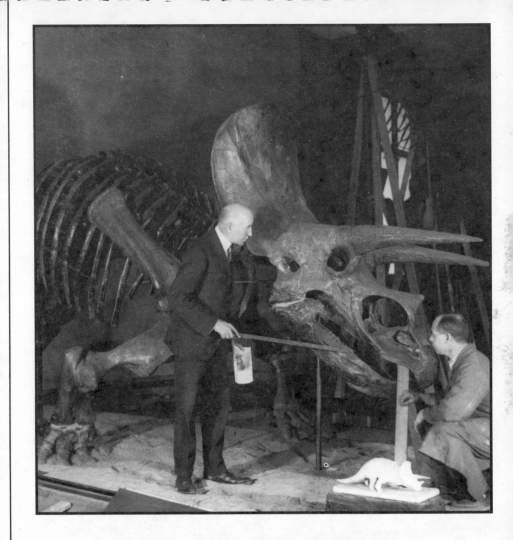

After that, other huge bones were discovered. It was clear that these bones all belonged to the same group of animals. An expert named the animals "dinosaurs."

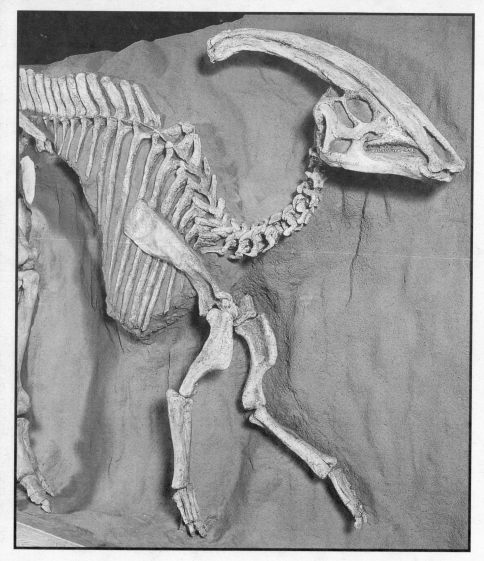

Since then people have uncovered many dinosaur bones. About six new kinds of dinosaurs are discovered every year!

Soon the dinosaur is put together. Then it is put on display for people to see.

What have we learned from dinosaur bones? Almost everything we know about dinosaurs!

There, experts unpack and clean
each bone. Then they rebuild the
dinosaur. They try to put each bone
in the right place.

Sometimes, bones are missing.
Experts make fake bones with
plaster or plastic to fill in the spaces.

Experts look for dinosaur bones
where wind or water has worn away
the land. In these places, they can
see layers of the Earth from long,
long ago.

Experts uncover bones by
removing the rock above them.
Or, they remove the whole
chunk of rock with the bones.

They wrap up the bones and rock.
They don't want anything to break!
Then the bones are shipped along to
a lab.

Scott Foresman
Reading

Grade 2
Phonics Reader 26

**Herbie and the
Donkey**
by Ada Evelyn
illustrated by
Don Peterson

Phonics Skills:
• Long *e* spelled *ie, ey*
• Consonant patterns
  gh, ph, lf/f/

Scott Foresman
**Phonics
System**

Scott Foresman

Herbie and
the Donkey

by Ada Evelyn
illustrated by Don Peterson

This book belongs to

_____

And he got a great new pal too.
"EEE-AWW!" the donkey agreed.

Herbie and the Donkey

by Ada Evelyn
illustrated by Don Peterson

Scott Foresman

Editorial Offices: Glenview, Illinois • New York, New York
Sales Offices: Reading, Massachusetts • Duluth, Georgia
Glenview, Illinois • Carrollton, Texas • Menlo Park, California

Herbie Fox needed money. He wanted to get himself a cool new bike. But he didn't want to work. Not Herbie!

© Scott Foresman 2

"I won't," said his dad. "You worked hard for that money. Then you used it to help your donkey. Now I'm going to help you."

They walked together to the bike store. Herbie got his cool new bike after all.

"Is that what you got with all that money you made?" asked Herbie's dad. "Herbie Fox, if you want a bike ...."

"Please!" Herbie said. "Don't tell me to get another job!"

14

Herbie looked in a chair. He found two pennies, a toy elephant, and a few cookie crumbs.

"What are you doing?" his dad asked.

"I'm looking for money," Herbie told him. "I need a new bike."

His dad just laughed.

"Herbie," he said, "get a job!"

3

Herbie didn't like the sound of
that. But he didn't know what to do.
Then he saw a photograph. It was
above an ad in the paper.
DONKEY
FREE TO GOOD HOME
Call 555-5252

4

"What are you doing now?" Herbie's
dad asked.

"I'm putting new sneakers on my
donkey," Herbie said.

13

Herbie raked a few leaves. Then
he raked a few more leaves!
　　He kept all the money he made.
Finally, he had enough.

"A donkey!" Herbie said.
"A donkey is cooler than a bike!"
　　He called the number. Then he
went to see the donkey.

"Do you want to come home with me?" Herbie asked.

"EEE-AWW!" the donkey said.

It was a terrible sound. But Herbie decided it must mean yes.

6

Herbie found a number of jobs. He painted the numbers on Suzie Bean's house. He walked Jamie Harvey's rough and tough dog.

11

Herbie dragged his donkey home.
He kept thinking about what to do.
"I'm stuck," he said. "Now I have to
get a job!"

The next day, a few foxes were
going for a bike ride. Herbie rode
his new donkey.

He couldn't believe it. He kept
falling behind. The donkey would
not run. In fact, he didn't even like
to walk.

The donkey sat down in a field halfway home. "What's the matter with you?" Herbie asked.

The donkey held one leg above his head. Herbie looked. He said, "No wonder you didn't want to run! Your feet are red and sore."

Scott Foresman
Reading

Grade 2
Phonics Reader 27

**The Shoemaker
and the Elves**
retold by Stacey Sparks
illustrated by
Philip Smith

Phonics Skills:
• Long e spelled *ei*
• Plural *es* (changing
  f to *v* before adding)

Scott Foresman
Phonics
System

Scott Foresman

The Shoemaker
and the Elves

retold by Stacey Sparks
illustrated by Philip Smith

This book belongs to

_____

Phonics for Families: This book gives your child practice in reading words with long *e* spelled *ei,* as in *neither;* words in which the final *f* is changed to a *v* before adding *-es,* as in *elves;* and the high-frequency words *eight, road, round, start,* and *young.* Read the book together. Then have your child find words in the book with long *e* spelled *ei.*

Phonics Skills: Long *e* spelled *ei;* Plural *-es* (changing *f* to *v* before adding)

High-Frequency Words: *eight, road, round, start, young*

The elves never came back. But the
shoemaker and his wife were fine. They
had enough gold for the rest of their
lives. And they had two other little
people to care for!

The Shoemaker and the Elves

retold by Stacey Sparks
illustrated by Philip Smith

Scott Foresman

Editorial Offices: Glenview, Illinois • New York, New York
Sales Offices: Reading, Massachusetts • Duluth, Georgia
Glenview, Illinois • Carrollton, Texas • Menlo Park, California

Once there was a shoemaker. He lived with his wife in a little shop. The man made good shoes, but he was poor. Sometimes he had no gold to buy leather.

"You look great!" said one elf.
"You do too!" said the other.
"We are such fine little men," said the elves. "Let's go out and have some fun!"
And they ran out the door and down the road!

That night the elves came out again.
They got up on the table.

"Look!" cried the elves. "Real clothes
for us!"

They got dressed quickly.

The shoemaker and his wife had no
children. They lived by themselves. At
least that's what they thought.

Neither one knew that two young
elves lived in the shop too.

All day long, the elves sat in the attic above the ceiling. Each day, they peeped down through a hole. They liked to watch the man make shoes.

At night, the elves came out to look for food.

© Scott Foresman 2

"I know!" said his wife. "I will make them new clothes. They must be very cold with just leaves on."

The next day she worked very hard. She made two little hats. She made two tiny jackets. She made two little pairs of pants.

That night, the shoemaker and his wife climbed up to the attic. They peeped down through the hole.

"Elves!" cried the shoemaker. "Look how fast they work! And neither of us has thanked them."

"How can we thank them?" asked his wife.

One day the shoemaker went out to buy some leather. He brought home just enough to make one pair of shoes. He cut it into two neat pieces.

At eight o'clock, he felt sleepy. "I think I will make the shoes tomorrow," he said. "I'm tired. I need to go to bed."

After the shoemaker went to bed, the elves came out. They ran along the shelves looking for crumbs. They tipped over a cup and a few drops of milk spilled out. They drank the milk.

Still hungry, they grabbed the rungs of the chairs and climbed up onto the table.

© Scott Foresman 2

Time passed. The shoemaker and his wife grew rich.

"Life is good," said the wife. "But I wish we knew who was helping us. I would like to say thank you."

Then she thought of a plan.

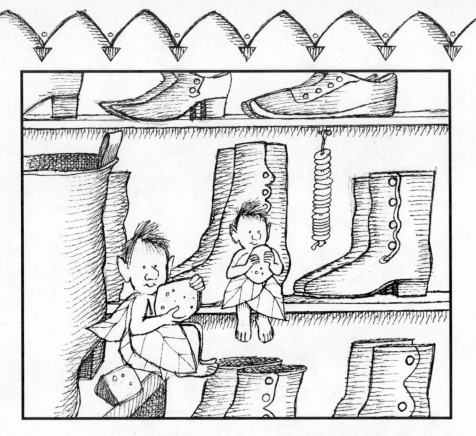

The shoemaker cut the leather. When he went to bed, the elves came out. Again they made fine shoes. The shoemaker sold the shoes for a good price. Then he bought enough leather for four more pairs of shoes. He also bought two round loaves of bread. That night the elves had a feast!

"Here are two big pieces of meat!" cried one elf.

Then he got closer. "No," he said sadly. "It's just leather for more shoes."

"I think we should help the poor shoemaker," said the other elf. "After all, we live in his house and eat his food."

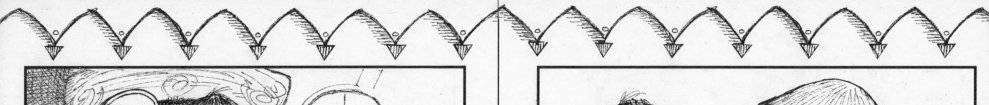

Next morning, the shoemaker was ready to start work. He went to his table.

"Look!" he called to his wife. "Look at these fine shoes!"

"Who made them?" she asked.

"I don't know," he said.

"I don't know either," she cried.

8

Just then a rich man came to the shop. He saw the shoes the elves had made.

"What fine shoes!" he said. "I want to buy them!"

The shoemaker received enough gold to buy leather for two more pairs of shoes!

© Scott Foresman 2

9

Scott Foresman
Reading

Grade 2
Phonics Reader 28

Little Book of Bridges
by Judy Veramendi
illustrated by
Jack Crane

Phonics Skills:
- *R*-controlled vowels
  (*air, are*)
- Consonant pattern *dge*
  /j/

Scott Foresman
Phonics
System

Scott Foresman

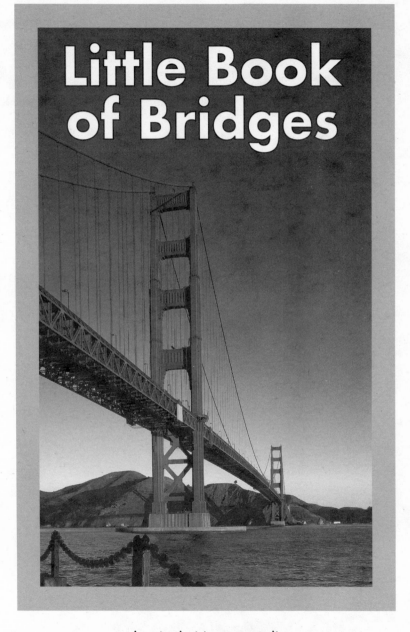

Little Book of Bridges

by Judy Veramendi
illustrated by Jack Crane

This book belongs to

_____

Phonics for Families: This book gives your child practice in reading words that have the same vowel sound heard in *pair* and *care;* words with the letters *dge;* and the high-frequency words *add, any, both,* and *mean.* Read the book with your child. Then ask your child to find all the words in the story that rhyme with *stare.*

Phonics Skills: *R*-controlled vowels (*air, are*); Consonant pattern *dge* /j/

High-Frequency Words: *add, any, both, mean*

When you cross a bridge, do you think about how it was made or who made it? Next time you cross a bridge, look at it closely. Look to see if it is like any of the bridges in this book.

16

Little Book of Bridges

by Judy Veramendi
illustrated by Jack Crane

Scott Foresman

Editorial Offices: Glenview, Illinois • New York, New York
Sales Offices: Reading, Massachusetts • Duluth, Georgia
Glenview, Illinois • Carrollton, Texas • Menlo Park, California

Bridges trace outlines against the sky. They stand tall against fair, blue skies and stormy, gray skies.

Large cables are pulled across the river. These cables hold up the bridge. It takes people from edge to edge—across the river.

One rare kind of bridge can be found in Ecuador. It is called a "hanging bridge." It is made of cables strung high across a river.

Old stone bridges were made across streams and rivers. People long, long ago would add stone upon stone to make bridges like this one.

Old bridges are both useful and beautiful. On a nice day, the sun glares off the stones of these bridges.

For thousands of years little bare feet have walked across these bridges, barely moving the dust.

4

If you stood on this bridge and stared up at the cables, you might feel a little scared. But you shouldn't be afraid. The cables of this bridge hang from great towers wedged deeply into the bottom of the bay.

13

Not all bridges that go over water are low. In fact, some are very high over the water. They hang from cables. Cars, trailers, or trucks can cross these bridges.

Many pairs of boots have pounded the stones. Carts have rolled across these bridges. And now, cars move across them.

Some very old bridges were made to carry water from the hills to the cities. These tall bridges do not carry any water today.

6

This might mean that you should give yourself more time if you have to cross one of these bridges. You never know! You might have to wait for a tall ship to pass.

11

Some bridges go across valleys. Some go across roads. And others go across water.

Some bridges must open to let tall ships by. When bridges split, cars have to wait to cross the bridge.

But they still stand in towns, cities, and countrysides. Some are more than two thousand years old. They remind us of how people used to live.

Long ago, some small bridges went over land far below. The people who crossed them every day were not scared. They did not care if the bridge swayed a bit.

But if you set foot on one of these bridges, you might care. You might be a little scared. You might say to the bridge, "Please do not budge."

Scott Foresman
Reading

Grade 2
Phonics Reader 29

**The Broken Radio
Jug Band**
by Susan McCloskey
illustrated by
Mike Dammer

Phonics Skills:
- Long vowels at the ends
  of syllables
- Consonants *ch/k/* and
  sch/sk/

Scott Foresman
Phon✶cs
System

Scott Foresman

The Broken
Radio Jug Band

by Susan McCloskey
illustrated by Mike Dammer

This book belongs to

_____

Phonics for Families: This book gives your child practice in reading words with long vowels at the ends of syllables, as in *tiger* and *Zena;* words with the *k* sound spelled *ch,* as in *chorus;* words with the *sk* sound spelled *sch,* as in *school,* and the high-frequency words *also, group, soon, though,* and *tried.* Read the book together. Then ask your child to talk about the kinds of music he or she likes.

Phonics Skills: Long vowels at the ends of syllables; Consonants *ch/k/* and *sch/sk/*

High-Frequency Words: *also, group, soon, though, tried*

Zena's broken radio finally did get fixed. Zena and her friends got together every weekend to hear beautiful music.

But sometimes the music came from the radio. And other times it came from the Broken Radio Jug Band!

16

The Broken Radio Jug Band

by Susan McCloskey
illustrated by Mike Dammer

Scott Foresman

Editorial Offices: Glenview, Illinois • New York, New York
Sales Offices: Reading, Massachusetts • Duluth, Georgia
Glenview, Illinois • Carrollton, Texas • Menlo Park, California

Zena almost cried. She had
dropped her radio and it had broken
into tiny pieces. Who could fix it?
Maybe Leo can fix it. Zena called him
right away.

2

© Scott Foresman 2

Soon most of the animals were
clapping and singing along with the
music. Those that weren't clapping
and singing were dancing.

15

Tracey made a deep sound by blowing into a jug. It sounded as if a train were going by. That's when the frog chorus began to sing.

"It's no use, Zena," said Leo. "I've tried and tried. I just don't know where this piece goes."

Zena sighed. Without that piece, the radio won't work. And without a radio, there can't be music tonight at the party.

"We can still have tasty snacks tonight," said Leo.

"And we can still play games," said Zena.

"But we won't have music," said Leo.

Then Leo got an idea. "Hmm. Maybe we will," he said to himself.

Zena's mouth opened wide when the music began. She had never heard anything like it before.

Chris tapped a tin cup with a spoon. Tony scraped out a quick tune with an old washboard and a stick. Grover joined in by blowing on a comb with paper.

Just then Leo spoke up. "However," he said, "there is also happy news. We will still be able to hear music. Please put your hands together for the Broken Radio Jug Band!"

Leo told Chris about his idea. Chris said, "It's not as crazy as it sounds. I used to play the piano. I don't have a piano anymore, but I do have some tin cups and spoons. I bet I can still make music."

"Good!" said Leo. "Don't tell Zena, though. We will surprise her."

Then Leo and Chris talked to Tony. Tony said, "I used to make music with a stick and my mom's washboard. I bet I can still make music."

"Good!" they said. "Don't tell Zena, though. We will surprise her."

6

Finally, the time Zena had been dreading arrived. She stood up before her friends.

"Dear friends," she began. "I have sad news. We won't be able to hear music on the radio tonight."

11

That night the animals went to Zena's party. Zena had made her friends a tasty snack. They all ate until their stomachs were full. Later they all played a game of "Pin the Hat on the Man."

Leo, Chris, and Tony talked to Grover. Grover said, "My friend Ann used to make music with a comb and some paper. I can do that!"

"Good!" they said. "Don't tell Zena, though. We will surprise her."

Next the animals talked to Tracey.
Tracey said, "I used to like to blow
into a jug. It sounded like music to me.
I can still do that!"

"Good!" they said. "Don't tell Zena,
though. We will surprise her."

Then the animals told some frogs
about their idea.

One frog said, "I sang in a choir in
school. I can help these other frogs sing."

"Good!" they said. "Don't tell Zena,
though. We will surprise her."

Scott Foresman
Reading

Grade 2
Phonics Reader 30

Our Vacation
by Sharon Fear
illustrated by
Dave Joly

Phonics Skills:
- *R*-controlled vowels
  (*ear*/ėr/, *our*/our/)
- Syllable pattern *tion*

Scott Foresman
Phonics System

Scott Foresman

Our Vacation

by Sharon Fear
illustrated by Dave Joly

This book belongs to

_____

Phonics for Families: This book features words that contain the vowel sounds heard in *earn* and *sour*; words with the letters *tion*, as in *vacation*; and the high-frequency words *already*, *buy*, *nothing*, *piece*, and *used*. Read the book with your child. Then have your child find all the words in the story with *tion*.

Phonics Skills: *R*-controlled vowels (ear/ėr/, our/our/; Syllable pattern *tion*

High-Frequency Words: *already*, *buy*, *nothing*, *piece*, *used*

We never did go on vacation. But it didn't matter. As Mom said, our vacation came to us!

Our Vacation

by Sharon Fear
illustrated by Dave Joly

Scott Foresman

Editorial Offices: Glenview, Illinois • New York, New York
Sales Offices: Reading, Massachusetts • Duluth, Georgia
Glenview, Illinois • Carrollton, Texas • Menlo Park, California

Our vacation was almost planned. We were going to Iceland. All we needed to do was decide how we were going to get there. Mom checked the screen.

© Scott Foresman 2

"And you," she said to Dad. "Be a good host. Pass the snacks. I'm going to join the party."
Then she smiled.

Mom fought her way to the beamer. She gave it a sour look and then hit the OFF button.

She looked at me and said, "Order some food. And don't forget to order food for the dogs and the elephant."

Then she asked my brother to rent about fifty sleeping bags.

"We could take the speed train to New York. And then take the tunnel to Iceland," said Mom.

"That could take an hour or more," said my brother. "Isn't there anything faster?"

"What about the beamer?" I said.

"Beamer" isn't its real name.
But that's what everyone calls it.
It beams you to any other beamer
station on Earth in just seconds. It's
the newest thing in transportation.
Nothing is faster!

4

"My beamer!" cried Dad.
"My rug!" cried Mom.
"What strange reactions!"
I thought.

13

But it was not hard to miss the next thing coming out. It was the most amazing thing I had ever seen. It was a man on a huge elephant!

"Too late," said Mom after searching the screen. "It's already sold out. You have to buy beamer time very early. I've heard there are always lines at the station."

Just then Dad came in with two other people. They were carrying bits and pieces of something. "No lines for us," Dad said.

The people snapped each piece together. Then they plugged it in. And there was a beamer!

"Our own beamer!" said Dad. "This will beam us . . . "

"Any place on Earth in seconds!" my brother and I said at the same time. We had heard the ads many, many times.

© Scott Foresman 2

"Look out!" Dad yelled. I jumped back just as two teams of dog sleds came racing in.

There was so much going on at our place. It was hard to see everything!

Then people started coming quickly. First came a chef. Then came an astronaut. Clowns in motion followed the chef and astronaut. They leaped and tumbled into the room.

"We can't buy a beamer! We don't earn enough!" said Mom.

"It is slightly used," said Dad. "It was used just once. A lady used it to visit her great-grandchildren in Hong Kong."

Dad reached for the ON button. "Wait," I said. "Maybe we should read how to use it first." But I spoke up too late. The beamer had already started to hum.

8

"Which way to the beach?" asked a tanned surfer. He had just hopped out of the beamer and was grinning at us.

Another hum, and out popped a lady in a ski outfit. "How's the snow?" she asked.

9